The Reaffirmation of Prayer

The
Reaffirmation
of
Prayer

E. Glenn Hinson

BROADMAN PRESS
Nashville, Tennessee

Scripture quotations marked (RSV) are from the Revised Standard
Version of the Bible, copyrighted 1946, 1952, © 1971, 1973.

© Copyright 1979 • Broadman Press
All rights reserved.

4219-47
ISBN: 0-8054-1947-0

Dewey Decimal Classification: 248.3
Subject heading: PRAYER
Library of Congress Catalog Card Number: 78-66775
Printed in the United States of America.

To
Douglas V. Steere
Friend and Spiritual Mentor

Contents

Preface

This book has grown out of a paper entitled "Prayer in an Economy of Abundance" which I delivered several years ago to the Ecumenical Institute of Spirituality. In that paper, published in *Religion in Life* in the autumn of 1975, I pointed out that, in our affluent society, prayer may be seen as an alien and even as an enemy. It is an alien in the sense that this distracted and fast-paced society neither encourages nor leaves room for prayer. It is an enemy in the sense that it erodes an economy predicated on overconsumption and waste. In the conclusion of this paper I expressed a bit more optimism about prayer in this setting, arguing that it can be a friend—not of the economy of abundance but of all humankind—by bringing us into contact with the God of all.

Prayer as a friend of humankind is the chief concern

of this book. In it I have tried to show how we may apply the traditional dimensions or forms of prayer both critically and constructively to our contemporary situation in the United States.

As I see it, the problem of prayer is chiefly a problem of faith. Consequently, I have begun this book with a serious effort to deal with the dimension of praise. If we render that praise to God for which, as Augustine says, he made us, then prayer and all the dimensions of prayer make sense. If we cannot praise God, not merely with our lips but with our hearts, then prayer means nothing and forms do not matter.

The rest of the book is a call for full-bodied prayer which use of traditional dimensions or forms of prayer may help us recover. What matters, of course, is not the forms but prayer itself, namely conversation, communion, or communication between ourselves as personal beings and God, the heavenly Father, as the ultimate personal reality in the universe. What matters further is how this engagement with God carries over into all dimensions of our personal lives and our society.

Forms, then, are secondary to the main concern. Insofar as they can help us in this dual engagement, with God and with our world, they deserve serious renewed attention. As in the past, forms can keep us from narrow, one-sided, and self-centered perspectives which so readily intrude into our conversation with God. They can help us see the world, as it were, through God's eyes.

Although surrender is not one of the traditional dimensions, I have included a chapter on it. This is based on the theological judgment, surely in line with Jesus' own teaching and experience, that the most truly Christian prayer is one which puts all things, including one's own life, in God's hands. The central article in our prayer is always that his kingdom may come and his will be done on earth as in heaven.

I hope that you will find reading this book a searching, and even a disturbing, experience. Despite the reassurance which you may find in my emphasis on traditional forms, the application of these to our situation poses some uncomfortable questions about life in the economy of abundance, even life in the "comfortable pews" of many churches. I am proposing that we bring these queries directly into both our private and our public prayer. Anything less would make a mockery of prayer, nay, of faith itself.

You can quickly discover what I am getting at in this book by turning to the litany I have put together in chapter 7. This litany, designed for public worship, can be used as it stands in certain services, but it was intended to serve as a guide for constructing prayers. It incorporates many of those concerns which we, in the economy of abundance, need to awaken in our private and corporate consciousness. In using it, therefore, you will want to pay attention to *content* rather than form. Every article in each of its sections can be particularized and expanded, thus enhancing its applicability.

I am quite conscious that some of my readers strongly

influenced by the anti- or nonliturgical Puritan tradition, may feel somewhat uncomfortable with the stress
I have placed in this book on self-conscious attention
to prayer, whether public or private. This tradition
has emphasized spontaneity in prayer and worship, by
which is often meant unpreparedness. The Spirit is
supposed to work better off the top of our heads, as
it were.

Although I fully understand the original motive for
the Puritan attitude, namely, to get away from wooden
liturgical prayers recited without thought or feeling;
I believe we must now openly reexamine it. Has the
emphasis on spontaneity not led in practice to wooden
liturgical prayers recited without thought or feeling,
even though not written down? Do so-called spontaneous prayers not mouth the same trite and meaningless
phrases week by week? Unless some crisis interrupts
to create a new focus of prayer, the answer is yes in
both cases. Anyone who has frequented Baptist worship services knows how accurate this is. What we find
all too often are liturgical prayers of very poor quality.
The prayers of great liturgies at least possess thoughtful
and carefully formulated elements, even when passage
of time dates them a great deal.

Please understand, I am not calling for *formal* liturgical prayers but rather for the *deepening* of prayer
through self-conscious effort. Deepening will necessitate *preparation* for public prayer. This preparation
could include several ingredients. One is private
prayer, always an essential for effective corporate wor-

ship. Another is the corporate prayer of leaders of worship which will deepen and expand their perceptions. Every church staff should pray together, not for programmatic reasons but because they are conscious of their own relationship to God and the weighty task he has allotted them. A third ingredient is careful and self-conscious attention to prayers which will be used in public worship, whether said spontaneously, read, sung, or recited antiphonally. The issue here is: Does the Holy Spirit not work as well through a longer, self-conscious process as through a momentary one? Logic compels us to say yes indeed.

I am indebted to many persons, both living and dead, for the content of this book. Some debts are acknowledged by notes, others are not. I would express special appreciation to the Ecumenical Institute of Spirituality and Douglas Steere, one of its founders, for an extraordinary stimulus regarding the topic discussed. I am grateful to God for the ecumenical winds which have blown across our globe from John XXIII's accession in 1958 and refreshed all of Christendom. How all Christians should rejoice that, after centuries of polemic and recrimination, we can again appreciate our rich common heritage of prayer! At last all—Catholic, Protestant, Orthodox—can claim the whole heritage as our own.

E. GLENN HINSON

1

The
Recovery
of
Dimensions
of
Prayer

This book is devoted to a reconsideration of the traditional forms or dimensions of prayer: praise or adoration, thanksgiving, confession, intercession, petition, and dedication. It is based on the assumption that these forms, vital throughout the history of Christianity, still have relevance in our day. The query that some have raised about them and that has caused them to fall into disuse sometimes today is not one of applicability. Rather, like so many other elements of Christian observance, the problem has to do with adaptation. All too often, forms such as these are applied to yesterday's thought patterns and contexts and not updated to relate Christian faith to those of today and tomorrow.

This is not to say that *all* elements of tradition remain relevant and useful. Many do belong only to the past, suitable for study by historians but not worthy of being emulated in the present. Who, for example, would insist on holding on to all the creeds of Christian history with their often contradictory clauses and purposes? Or all of the organizational patterns? The churches need not feel bound to particular forms, and the history of Christianity attests readily enough that historical conditioning has occurred in all of them. To discard some forms boldly is the better part of wisdom.

It is wise also, however, to distinguish between forms. The fact that *some* no longer apply to our situation does not mean *all* are irrelevant. Such seems to me to be especially true of the traditional forms of prayer discussed in this book. These, to be sure, are not to be confused with prayer itself. Prayer itself is conversation, communication, or communion between ourselves as personal beings and our heavenly Father, the ultimate personal reality in the universe. These facets help us develop well-rounded communication and avert the self-centeredness which so often characterizes Protestant prayer.

The so-called spontaneous style of Protestant prayer is especially liable to lapse into a one-dimensional style, namely petition. The focus falls on those who pray— not on God, or on the two-way conversation with him. "Give . . . help . . . do for us" is the overworked refrain of spoiled and selfish children who have too little concern for their heavenly Father and his desires for them and too much for themselves and their wants.

The traditional forms of prayer supply us with disciplines to improve our conversation with the heavenly

Father, whether in public or in private. They could be viewed, as it were, as the pattern which we imprint on our minds and hearts to assure intelligent and mature dialogue. I am not suggesting, of course, that we will simply click off each of these aspects like points on an outline. Prayer, in the final analysis, ought to be natural and spontaneous, like our conversation with other human beings. If you will reflect for a moment on the way in which you developed your present conversation patterns, however, you will recognize the part played by certain oft-repeated forms and devices designed to foster more mature and well-rounded speech. You recited poems. You diagrammed sentences. You memorized great speeches and classic passages from the Bible or other great literature. You studied rhetorical devices. You examined others' outlines. Altogether, combined with natural speech endowment, such exercises equipped you for natural and spontaneous speech. Once drilled into your thought processes, they were relegated to your subconscious, coming into play automatically in ordinary speech.

The analogy of speech-conditioning exercises helps us only partially, for prayer differs from ordinary conversation. In its truest sense it takes us beyond words and thoughts and set patterns of speech and engages us in a direct exchange of love energies. Heart speaks to heart. The Spirit himself comes to our aid (Rom. 8:26).

What is involved here actually is communion, which, as in human friendships, depends on inward disposition and orientation rather than words or other symbols. The formation of inward disposition also requires training in which certain maxims may play a pivotal role. Deeply imprinted on the subconscious by repetition, such maxims generate conditioned reflexes which are triggered in encounters with other persons in various situations. Certain physical postures, for instance, such as folding the hands, closing the eyes, bowing the head, and kneeling, condition us for prayer. When we first did these, perhaps as infants, they meant little and they did little to ready us for prayer. In time, however, prayer reflexes developed in response to the physical disciplines. In a similar way, the traditional prayer forms gradually build reflexes of praise, thanksgiving, confession, intercession, petition, and dedication—attitudes crucial to genuine engagement with the heavenly Father.

Subsequent chapters will explore case histories of the disappearance of such attitudes from the modern mentality and reflect on strategies to recover them. At the moment, however, it might be worthwhile to ask whether they are recoverable. Many might say no. "Modern man," we heard often in the sixties, is characterized by a profound sense of God's absence. A sense of his presence is not recoverable without turning the clock back to an earlier day to restore the life-style which accompanied belief.

Whether such a conclusion is correct depends to a large degree on where we locate the cause of the experience of absence. If it lies in the fact that there is no God or that he no longer exists or that he has hidden himself from us, then these may not be recoverable. If, however, it lies in the fact that human beings, for varied reasons, have ceased to inculcate attitudes of praise, thanksgiving, and all the others, then we *can* work toward their recovery. What is needed is reeducation or, perhaps more precisely, therapy to restore shrunken sensitivities to the Other. The traditional forms could serve, as it were, as the exercises which will help withered spiritual perceptions regain the vibrancy lost by disuse. Here we might learn by looking into the past to see why and how prayer forms were used.

Dimensions of Prayer in the New Testament

The first Christian to outline the forms of prayer being discussed here is Origen (185-255), the first systematic theologian and one of the most eminent and creative biblical scholars of all time. In his treatise *On Prayer* (14), however, he was alluding to 1 Timothy 2:1 f.: "I urge you, therefore, first of all to make entreaties, prayers, intercessions, and thanksgivings for all persons, for rulers and all who are in places of authority that we may lead a quiet and tranquil life in complete piety and reverence" (author's translation.)

We should exercise caution in making clearcut distinctions between words listed in a series such as this because early Christian writers of Jewish background often applied this technique simply to reinforce their point. In this case the chief point is that Christians ought to pray for *all* persons, not merely fellow Christians, and especially for persons in government, for if the latter establish a peaceful social structure, they benefit worship of God. The distinctions between dimensions of prayer are incidental to this point.

At the same time, the different words used here appear often enough with different nuances in early Christian writings to show that some distinctions were being made. The word translated "prayers," *proseuche,* is the most comprehensive and commonly used word, and either in a verb or a noun form, it embraces all the others. Often, as in Philippians 4:6 and Colossians 4:2, it is itself nuanced with other words such as "thanksgiving." Therefore, we cannot ascribe a special nuance to it as we may to the other three.

The word translated "entreaties," *deesis,* has a somewhat more specific nuance, but often it paralleled *proseuche* more or less closely (see Eph. 6:18; Phil. 4:6). Insofar as it was distinguished, it was used either in verb or noun forms to depict the act of begging, pleading, petitioning, or fervent asking which one person directs to another or to God.

The word translated "intercessions," *enteuxis,* is a still more precise term. In both verb and noun forms it designated the act of serving as a go-between, whether between one human being and another or between a human being and God. In Romans 8:26 ff. Paul posits this intercessory role in the Spirit. The Spirit comes to our aid in our impotence as human beings.

"For," says the apostle, "we don't know what we must pray for. But the Spirit himself intercedes *(hyperentuchano)* with unspeakable groanings. And he who examines our hearts knows the Spirit's thought, because (that) he intercedes on behalf of the saints."

The word translated "thanksgivings," *eucharistia,* is likewise quite distinct from the general term *proseuche,* as its frequent usage to qualify the latter shows (Phil. 4:6; 1 Tim. 4:3 f.; Col. 4:2). It usually designated an *attitude* of mind and heart in which the believer should approach God. Paul, for instance, enjoined the Philippians to let their requests in entreaty and prayer be issued "with thanksgiving" (Phil. 4:6). It is hardly surprising that the central Christian observance of worship, the Lord's Supper, came early to be called a "eucharistia" (1 Cor. 10:16; *Didache* 9:1, 5; Ignatius, *Ephesians* 13:1; *Philadephians* 4).

In addition to these four terms, we find several others used to designate dimensions of prayer. One of these is praise, *doxa, doxazo.* Praise, like thanksgiving (see Rom. 1:21, where the two are paralleled), is a natural and spontaneous response to an experience of love, concern, and help. In the Gospels we find numerous examples of ascriptions of praise to God as people experienced or witnessed miracles of healing performed by Jesus (Matt. 9:8; 15:31; Mark 2:12; Luke 5:25 f.; 7:16; 13:13; 17:15; 18:43; 23:47). Jesus himself urged his hearers to do good deeds that people might praise God in seeing them (Matt. 5:16). In Acts 11:18; 21:20, Luke connected outbursts of praise with the reports of success in the early church's missionary endeavors. For Paul, the aim of circumspect Christian behavior and effort, especially the harmony of Jews and Gentiles (Rom. 15:6,9), was praise of God.

Another dimension of prayer is confession, *exhomologesis*. Confession is based on the thoroughly biblical recognition of human sinfulness and frailty. The Old Testament Psalms, as well as other Old Testament writings, are filled with confessional elements and entreaties for purification. Moreover, in one of his most memorable parables, conserved by Luke alone (Luke 18:9-14), Jesus defended his ministry to the outcasts and sinners by pointing to confession as a sign of authentic piety. The tax collector who could only strike his breast and cry out for God's mercy to himself as a sinner was far better off than the Pharisee who justified himself by fasting and tithing. Those who humble themselves, *God* will lift up; those who lift *themselves* up, he will humble (Luke 18:14; 14:11; Matt. 23:12). Confession became a regular part of Christian prayer and worship. Thus the author of the epistle of James urged: "If anyone of you has sinned, it will be forgiven to him (her). Therefore, confess your sins to one another and pray for one another that you may be healed. The prayer of a righteous person is able to do wonders" (5:15-16, author's translation). By A.D. 200 some churches had developed a formal public confession called the *exhomologesis*. Though it went far beyond the simple forms of early Christianity, the custom responded to a well-founded recognition that a proper relationship with God is dependent on an acknowledgment of sin and genuine repentance.

There may be numerous other dimensions of prayer, but the final one to which I will call attention here is surrender, dedication, or commitment. We have no specific word to designate this dimension of prayer. I base my observations about it on prayer in the Psalms and in the life of Jesus himself. In the last analysis this prayer is the one which expresses faith at its most profound level. It is the prayer of Gethsemane: "Abba, Father, you can do all things. Take this cup of suffering out of my hands. Yet don't do what I will but what you will" (Mark 14:36; John 5:30; 6:38, author's translation). It is the cry from the cross: "Father, into your hands I lay down my spirit" (Luke 23:46). Such an act of surrender is based on the discovery that, as the apostle Paul said, "neither death, nor life, angels nor principalities, nor things present, nor things to come, nor powers, nor heights, nor depths, nor any created thing can separate use from God's love which is in Christ Jesus, our Lord" (Rom. 8:38-39).

Recycling Our Understanding

We will return to these dimensions of prayer individually in subsequent chapters. For the moment I want to focus attention on the issue of education in prayer in its fuller dimensions.

We must face as candidly as we can the seriousness of the difficulty with this issue. We can begin to do so, of course, by recognizing that most persons pray for essentially selfish motives. They bring God in as a "very present help in time of trouble," which he surely is, but much of the rest of the time simply ignore him. To a considerable degree this is natural of human beings. All of us tend to call on other persons out of need rather than from deeper motives. But what is natural and human has been exaggerated in modern technological societies. In the latter we measure activities in terms of immediate usefulness. We become impatient with those which might promise only long-range benefits or seem altogether profitless. Accordingly, in our hurry to get results, we have quietly allowed many once-valued interpersonal activities to slip away: swapping stories with friends, leisurely reading and meditation, conversation with our families around the dinner table, and many others. We have also put prayer to the pragmatic test. If, like Transcendental Meditation, it relaxes us, improves our health, and makes us function better, then we will pray. If not, we will spend our time in other activities.

Unfortunately the churches, especially the nonliturgical ones, have done little to offset this problem. Most of us learn our prayer habits in public worship, for, save for religious orders, few of the churches instruct their members in the art of praying. Behind this phenomenon evidently lies the poorly founded assumption that Christians do not require instruction in prayer; they should do it automatically.

If my observations here are correct, then the starting point for a retreading of our prayer practice should be public worship. We are concerned, of course, not merely with a *conscious* but with a *subconscious* reformation of attitudes and habits in conversation with God. To reach this goal, however, we will have to begin where we are—on the surface. Those of us in nonliturgical traditions may learn something here from the great liturgies of Christian history. These liturgies have used repetition, if not of words at least of themes, to reinforce and deepen prayer. Several avenues for the recycling of understanding for prayer should be explored.

One is *the outline of the entire worship service.* A complete service ought to include all of the elements of prayer we have been discussing. This does not mean that we must have prayers representing each. Other elements of worship may contribute also. *Scripture readings* may embrace some of these dimensions of prayer, particularly if we read from the Psalms. *Hymns* are, by their very nature, essentially prayers, sung rather than said. They cover virtually the entire range of dimensions we are concerned to track into our subconscious. How could we do better praising God, for instance, than to sing Charles Wesley's, "O for a Thousand Tongues to Sing," or giving thanks to God than to sing Martin Rinkart's "Now Thank We All Our God"? How could we do better confessing our sins than to sing John Newton's "Amazing Grace," or interceding for ourselves or others than to sing Martin Luther's "A Mighty Fortress Is Our God," or dedicating ourselves to God's will and purpose than to sing Frank Mason North's "Where Cross the Crowded Ways of

Life"? Both the response to invitation and the offering may represent dedication in a special way.

In this case, however, the issue is one of *completeness*. Most of those who lead worship in churches where sermons are central, as among Baptists, tend to select Scriptures and hymns or even to express prayers which complement the sermon. Although that practice has some value for achieving the objective set by the sermon, it does detract from the completeness and well-roundedness of the entire service. One or two aspects of prayer or worship are strongly emphasized, the others neglected entirely. The element which almost invariably gets the chief stress is petition. Worship thus becomes a monologue from the human side rather than a dialogue in which we not only address God but also he addresses us.

As a matter of practical necessity, it would be wise to apply a checklist to the liturgies we prepare. There may be no particular order in which various dimensions of our engagement with God have to enter the picture. However, there is doubtless wisdom in following the order often used in the great liturgies of Christian history and reiterated in the order of chapters in this book. In the first place stand praise and thanksgiving. Emerging naturally from these ascriptions is confession. Only then, humbled before the Creator and Redeemer, are we ready to make intercession for others and to raise up our petitions. Our final act should be one of dedication and commitment, putting ourselves at God's disposal to accomplish his will in and through us in the world.

A second avenue through which we may work at recycling our prayer patterns and attitudes is *in the pattern of individual prayers.* Each prayer in public worship, to be sure, does not require each of the traditional dimensions. Indeed, that would be inappropriate as well as unnecessary in the case of special prayers, for example, before or after the collection of an offering or as a benediction. It would lengthen prayers unduly and divert attention from their real purpose.

The sentiment has grown within me, however, that every service should have one complete prayer, rounded out in all of these dimensions. In most churches this would be the *pastoral* prayer, but I wonder if the pastoral prayer should not be thought of as a *congregational* prayer. To do so, of course, it would not have to be said by the whole congregation; many pastors and lay persons can gather the sincere desires, hopes, and concerns of all present and articulate them in a beautiful way.

There are numerous ways to involve a congregation in such a prayer. At one time most persons in the free church tradition rejected most of these alternatives in favor of spontaneity; many still do so. The concern which lay behind this, namely, sincerity, was a legitimate one, for liturgical prayers were often said without deep and meaningful engagement with God. Many now realize, however, that spontaneous prayers do not assure genuine worship. On the contrary, the price of spontaneity is often stereotyped prayers of far poorer quality than the great liturgical prayers of the past. Anyone who has listened attentively and tried to enter deeply into the worship of many Southern Baptist congregations will readily think of illustrations.

Keeping our instructional task in view, would it not be wise to prepare some fully dimensioned prayers, deliberately calling attention to the varied elements, and print them in the Sunday bulletin for all to share?

This is not to suggest imitation of the Anglican *Book of Common Prayer.* On the contrary, by using an outline we would spend much time in prayer and study each week to prepare prayers which speak to our precise situations. Both the outline and the content will shape and mold our pattern of prayer as they express our deepest and most heartfelt concerns. Some, I realize, will argue that preparation may hamper the Spirit. In reply I would ask whether the Spirit speaks more powerfully in a spur of a moment's reflection or in a long and thoughtful one. To me the answer is self-evident. Prayer should not be a matter of rote repetition; neither should it be a hasty mumbling of words based on a moment's excitement.

Praying Without Ceasing

In the last chapter I will incorporate some prayer specimens for public worship along the lines I am suggesting. In the remaining portion of this chapter I want to talk about "praying without ceasing," something which the apostle Paul directed the Thessalonians to do (1 Thess. 5:17).

I've often wondered how one could fulfill Paul's directive. Hermits or monks with callouses on their knees did so, I once thought. But I realized that Paul could not have intended a hermitic or monastic existence for the Thessalonians. On the contrary, he warned that if they did not get to work, they would not eat (2 Thess. 3:10).

A few years ago, I discovered a much better interpretation in Thomas Kelly's classic, *A Testament of Devotion*. In this book Kelly reminds us that we live life on two levels—the level of activities and the level of the interior life. Some persons in modern societies may live life only on the first level. They engage in activity for activities' sake. They rush through life, hurried and frantic, without ever seeming to get anywhere.

But there is another, a deeper level, Kelly says. This is the level where, stilled and tranquil, we listen for God's whisper in the ear of the heart.

When we first become serious about our engagement with God as novices in faith, we will *alternate* between these two. Now we engage in activities—now we converse with God. It is possible, however, to do these simultaneously as we grow. While we engage in activities, we tune in on the deeper level too, like listening to a stereo as we work. Prayer *informs* our activities.

In the seventeenth century a Carmelite lay brother named Nicholas Hermann or Brother Lawrence made a similar discovery. A very simple person, Brother Lawrence found that the rigorous disciplines of the Carmelite order didn't really help him to commune with God. While washing dishes in the monastery kitchen, which he did for forty years, he learned that he could talk to the God of pots and pans and things. He labeled his formula "the practice of the presence of God." Stated another way, he learned how to maintain an attitude of attention to the presence of God.

This appears to me to be what we are striving for. We want God to become a living reality in all of life. If this is to happen, however, we will have to get a better grasp of what prayer is. Prayer is not just words and thoughts. True, in public prayer, we will *use* words and thoughts, but they are only vehicles; they are not prayer itself. Prayer, I repeat, is conversation, communication, communion between ourselves and God.

If this definition is correct, then prayer has *two* sides, not *one* as we often suppose. The side which we focus on is *telling*. Certainly telling is an element. Sometimes, perhaps precisely because we learn how to pray from public worship, it is seen as the only element.

The other side of prayer, which we often neglect, is *listening*. The Quakers, of course, have much to teach us here, for they, in their silent worship, have cultivated the inner ear. The Quaker challenge is marvelously set forth by Douglas Steere in his classic *On Listening to Another,* an exposition of the art of hearing the Other.

This book will be concerned with developing the capacity to hear God as well as to speak to him. It is based on the assumption that he is always beaming messages to us if only we will listen.

The psalmist reminds us that "the heavens declare the glory of God; and the firmament sheweth his handiwork" (Ps. 19:1, KJV). Jesus drew object lessons from nature. The birds, the lilies, even the hairs of our head have messages. He also heard God speak through persons and events. If only we knew how to look at life as God sees it, all of life could become a prayer. Why is that not so? And what can we do about it? Those will be the questions I will try to answer in the rest of this book.

2
Praise

The starting gate of prayer is praise or adoration of God. "Thou hast made us for Thyself, to praise Thee," Augustine once prayed *(Conf.* 1.1), "and our hearts are restless until they find rest in Thee." From such praise spring all the other dimensions of prayer. Without it they would be meaningless.

Unfortunately in Western society we are encountering a problem precisely at this critical point. In recent years Westerners, industrialized, secularized, and enveloped by a profusion of tragedies of their own making, have been giving testimony of a profound sense of the absence of God in their experience. It is the opinion of many that Friedrich Nietzsche correctly surmised our situation when he declared, "God is dead!"

If the impact of this experience were only a philosophical one, we who believe could probably dismiss it from our minds and continue our praise of God without great anxiety. But its impact is not merely philosophical; it is existential. It has resulted in a profound sense of meaninglessness and despair, even nihilism. Samuel Beckett, a Nobel prize-winning playwright, has depicted well the whole experience. In his best-known play, *Waiting for Godot,* the principal character waits for Godot (God), but Godot never comes. In many others, such as *End Game,* Beckett exposes the utter meaninglessness, the boredom of modern existence. In one play he has rubble piled on the stage to be stared at by the audience for fifteen minutes and then bulldozed away.

During the 1960s, the so-called "God is dead" theologians brought the stark reality of this situation within the church itself. As we will see, they varied in their prescriptions about our response, but they agreed in their description of this sobering phenomenon. Many moderners lack the sense of a transcendent personal reality in their lives, the experience of God as the source and cause of the existence of the universe and of our personal existence. How, then, can they offer praise to him?

The Experience of God's Absence

This question is a profound one with which we must wrestle seriously in this chapter. Whether prayer and worship can mean anything at all will depend on whether we can give some answer. It will not suffice to dismiss those who have raised the questions as a "misguided minority." All serious persons will recognize that the experience of secularity affects all of us.

In *The Modern Schism* Martin E. Marty has pointed out that this experience of godlessness or secularity, which has come of age since around 1850, has assumed varied forms in Europe, England, and America.[1] In Europe it has taken the form of "utter secularity." Religion is not only left out of the picture but treated with hostility too. In Nietzsche's words, "God is dead!" Thus we are on our own. We are free. We must now play god ourselves. In England the experience has taken the form of "mere secularity." God is not attacked so much as he is ignored. Religion is accorded a symbolic role, in the coronation of the queen and in matters of state, but the average person shrugs it off. The church did little in the people's struggle for rights as laborers in the industrial revolution, why should they trouble themselves with it now? In America the experience has taken the form of "controlled secularity." God and religion are assigned a place, mainly in the private sector of the individual's experience but to a limited extent also in public.

The most striking expression of the experience of God's absence has occurred within the church. Dietrich Bonhoeffer articulated what many others had been experiencing when he asked whether modern persons had not reached the point where they could or had to be without a God-hypothesis, whether religion has gone for good, whether people could get along just as well without religious forms. He was echoed by a host of others as the "God is dead" movement came alive in the sixties.[2] God, they were saying, is simply not a part of the "modern" person's experience.

The existence of this phenomenon should not require detailed documentation, for it has been exposed in all sorts of media. What is of more immediate concern to us is the reason for it. The explanation has been approached from opposite ends of the question, from the divine end and from the human end.

God the Problem

One way to view it is to see God as the problem. How God is the problem may be regarded from several different angles.

One angle says that the reason we do not experience God is because he does not exist and never has. Thus in 1927 Bertrand Russell boldly explained why he was not a Christian by rejecting the classical arguments for God's existence—the uncaused Cause, the natural-law argument, the argument from design, the moral argument of Kant, and the argument that God is needed to remedy the injustice of man's present life. He proceeded to ascribe the origin of the God-hypothesis to emotion, above all, the emotion of fear. "Fear is the basis of the whole thing—fear of the mysterious, fear of defeat, fear of death." [3] God was modeled after the oriental despot. Free and intelligent persons can dispense with the whole idea.

Another is to say, as Karl Barth[4] did in early writings, that the reason we do not experience God is because

God has withdrawn himself. God, the absolute sovereign, has hidden himself—*Deus absconditus.* He does not reveal himself in nature but only in his Word, Christ. We can only perceive him in Christ, and we do not perceive him now because we are not looking at Christ.

Barth's accentuation of God's transcendence led to a third explanation to which many persons gave serious attention for a time, that is, that God is dead. "God is dead" theology, however, divided into two camps. Only one of the two would fit into the category we are now considering. This group, represented by Thomas J. J. Altizer[5] and William Hamilton,[6] approached the problem from the Barthian angle, but they went on to explain how this withdrawal of God occurred and what its consequences are. They did not abandon altogether the possibility that God once existed. He did exist. However, as Nietzsche had postulated, he died. In "the fullness of time," as it were, he poured himself into the life of Jesus of Nazareth and perished with him. But that act became our liberation from the God-hypothesis. God, by his own self-destruction, has now freed human beings to be completely on their own.

We the Problem

It is not my purpose to undertake a detailed critique of the three approaches which posit God as the problem. The first two offer plausible explanations, the third a highly implausible one from the perspective of a theistic definition of God. The approach itself is, if nothing else, a bit presumptuous. Whether God is or is not, who are we to establish a case either for or against him and to describe his relation to his creation? The Scriptures, which will doubtless have to guide us, simply assume that God is and that the problem is not God but human beings. If we are able to discover where the problem lies, at any rate, it is likely that our perceptions will enable us to discover it with ourselves more readily than with a God whose *absence* we profess to experience.

The other approach ascribes the problem to human beings and, more particularly, to the society which they have created through science and technology. Thence, the other "God is dead" group alluded to earlier concentrated on description.[7] In primitive societies human beings did experience divine beings. They attributed the operation of nature and their own behavior to personal realities outside themselves. They felt helpless in the face of demonic realities, whether good or bad, and considered themselves more or less the pawns of fate. This perception of existence continued until the late Middle Ages. Western science, however, has changed perceptions to such an extent that modern persons can no longer experience God, and we had just as well stop trying to communicate in God-language. We now view our world in an impersonal way— as a "steady state" phenomenon—and we internalize our self-understanding. As far as modern experience, whether correct or not, is concerned, "God is dead."

Without accepting altogether the conclusion that the
loss of a sense of God's presence is permanent and
irremediable, others also connect the experience of absence with human beings. The problem is, Father
Alfred Delp wrote in his *Prison Meditations,* that the
powers of perception of human beings in Western society have atrophied because of nonuse.[8] Since the Re-
naissance, Westerners have been cultivating the rational
powers to the neglect of the intuitive ones. The industrial revolution and developments consequent to it
have produced a new life-style, a secular one, which
leaves God out of the picture as is exhibited in the
shrinking of the powers of transcendence.

The causes for the shrinking of the powers of transcendence are too complex to sort out fully here, but
four major causes merit brief comment.

One is simply that the powers of observation and
reason have been cultivated so extensively that the
intuitive have gone to seed. This imbalance is obviously
connected with the deliberate emphasis which we, for
commendable reasons, have given to science and technology. As a part of this emphasis, the university has
gradually undergone a vast shift from education in humanities to education in fields which promise a larger
immediate return. In 1960 federal stipends were dis-
tributed 40 percent to military research, 37 percent
to medical research, 20 percent to other sciences, 3
percent to social sciences, and nothing to humanities.[9]
Consequently, college students feel the crunch to
choose scientific and technological vocations because

it is either that or joblessness.

Connected with and underlying a loss of the sense of a personal God is a loss of our own sense of personhood. This is a result of certain depersonalizing effects of the secular city. Relating to other persons is sorely tried in the latter. We have not seen the full effects of urbanization, but perceptive observers of our civilization, such as Arnold Toynbee, warn that this society which we have created poses the greatest threat to our survival as persons.[10] Whereas nature chastised man with whips, Toynbee says in a biblical parody, this society is chastising man with scorpions. We have frequent and graphic reminders of this danger. World Series fans will remember the savage outburst of New York Mets fans against Pete Rose and the Cincinnati Reds after a fight between Rose and the Mets' darling, Bud Harrelson. Then, when the Mets won the fifth game, the fans went out of control, tearing the turf from the outfield. A Louisville psychologist who had lived in New York City ascribed this to the depersonalizing effects of that city. The same could be said of the refusal of forty persons to intervene and thus save the life of Kitty Genovese, or of a hundred persons to stop two youths from mugging a prominent New York City lawyer in broad daylight. Feeling for persons, the sense of the personal, has atrophied. Why not also the sense of transcendent, personal God?

Another element which no doubt underlies this same experience is the distance which we have put between ourselves and nature. In conquering nature, we have denatured ourselves. We have suppressed some natural and instinctive responses, among which may be the restlessness of a heart which seeks God. A Parisian psychologist, Pierre Bensoussan, has attributed abuse regarding drugs and alcohol to the blah life modern persons experience in their removal from nature. He posited a remedy in religion, not of a traditional sort necessarily but at least of some sort. Today there is a return to nature via weekend trips, retreats, and farming, but these do not fully satisfy a deeper human craving. Indeed, we may ask whether anything less than a recovery of our own true nature as human beings will achieve that.

Another is the experience of brutality, starkly attested in the Holocaust, the bombing of Hiroshima and Nagasaki, and other events. Many Jewish people are atheists or agnostics today because of the massacre of six million Jews by Hitler—"Where could God have been," they ask. "How could this happen? Where could those who believe in God have been, those who say they worship God?" For these persons all human history will be dated from the Holocaust. This awful tragedy marked the end of one era and the beginning of another.

The Experience of God's Presence

Having spent this much time on the experience of the absence of God and its causes, we should now proceed to ask *whether* and *how* we may recover the experience of his presence, the sense of awe and wonder before the Unseen. Our answer, of course, will depend on which we accept of the explanations given above regarding the experience of absence.

The first set of approaches would likely convince us that any effort to recover the experience is futile. The most dogmatic response in this direction would come, of course, from the stolid atheist. One should rely upon sensory observation and intellect and avoid altogether the fears of the occult exhibited by primitive societies.

Karl Barth, from the opposite direction, negated human search for God. The most we can do is to wait upon God and to hear his Word as delivered already in the Scriptures. Christianity must lay aside "religion," that is, human and cultural expressions of faith. It must hearken solely to the Word delivered in the Scriptures, for God is not going to let us treat him as *Deus ex machina*. He is the One who seeks us. Any search on our part to find him could be futile.

It was this view which prepared the road for "God is dead" theology, which furthered Barth's attack upon "religion." According to Bonhoeffer in his musings during imprisonment, God, by his absence, is teaching us to get along without him. He calls each of us, as he called Christ, to be "the man for others." True Christianity is "religionless." [11] Altizer and Hamilton and some other secular theologians brought this to practical expression. Allan R. Brockway has depicted the piety of this type of Christian in a book called *The Secular Saint*.[12] Christians are those who accept fully the profound godlessness of their situation. That is their faith.

Having witnessed the "death of God," they no longer search in a puerile way for experience of what was but no longer is. They do not need the church or other ecclesiastical forms, although they may still tolerate them. Rather, they bear witness in the ordinary, everyday world to their own faith in themselves.

From the point of view of its *description* of the contemporary human plight, secular theology had much to offer. It was its *prescription,* however, which had to be questioned. It assumed that the patient's ailment was untreatable and incurable. Thus it prescribed complete cessation of usage rather than therapy for an atrophied faculty.

Granted, the faculty by which Westerners perceive God may be well along the way in the process of degeneration. There are ample evidences of this fact. Nevertheless, two questions should be interjected here.

One question is whether our God-consciousness, if it belongs to our essential nature, can ever be totally effaced. Was Augustine wholly wrong when he prayed, "Thou hast made us for Thyself, to praise Thee, and our hearts are restless until they find rest in Thee"? Can science and technology and urban life-styles obliterate the *imago Dei?* Or, contrariwise, is it possible that much of the restlessness and turmoil of the present age, both internal and external, are signs of the homing instinct God has planted in us?

The other query has to do with the significance of some current signs of a search for the transcendent personal. The search is taking both conventional and unconventional forms—mysticism, Transcendental Meditation, yoga exercises, astrology, revival of old religious practices, adoption of oriental faiths, glossolalia to name a few. Even if these are said to prove nothing about God's existence, do they not say something about human need and capacity for experiencing the transcendent? Do they not offer eloquent confirmation that human beings cannot live by bread alone?

Often we discover our deepest needs under the covering of artificial and contrived ones only after we are in danger of losing them. I am writing these words in Bangalore, India, where I heard George Fernandes, the Indian minister of economy and industry, make the same point last week. Fernandes spent several months in prison during the restrictive rule of Indira Ghandi along with a quarter million other political prisoners. "When the people had bread," he remarked, "they learned they also needed freedom." Could this be what modern societies with their materialistic bent are discovering about the transcendent? Material abundance is not enough. We hunger and thirst for something more.

The implications of these signs prompt me to look at a second set of approaches for a solution to the problem of a loss of transcendence. The second group of "God is dead" theologians argued rather persuasively for *changes in language and forms,* and with this I think we can agree. The chief question is: How far do we go in our adaptation and accommodation? Is there any substantive element of the traditional which cannot and does not have to be surrendered? Must we, for example, give up all God-talk because moderners have trouble understanding it?

In trying to answer these questions it is helpful to note that the voices of many secular theologians have changed dramatically since the sixties. Harvey Cox, for instance, did a complete somersault between *The Secular City* (1965) and *The Feast of Fools* (1969). In the former he lauded with little reservation the secular life-style characterized by preference for anonymity, profanity, pragmatism, and individualism; in the latter he argued for a recovery of medieval fantasying and utopian dreaming. Stated another way, in the former he virtually equated the secular city or the process of secularization with the kingdom of God; in the latter he looked for a city which has not yet arrived. In addition, Cox has recently been hymning the many religious and quasi-religious movements now abroad, including oriental cults and neopentecostalism.

To get beyond the description of the problem which these theologians have offered and to find some solution to it, we need to talk about a third approach, namely, *therapy for an atrophied faculty*. For if the problem stems from a loss of the powers of transcendence due to (1) overdevelopment of the powers of reason and observation, (2) the depersonalizing effects of the secular city, (3) removal from nature and thus from nature's Creator, and (4) the brutalizing and dehumanizing of persons, then something should be done to correct or nullify these conditions.

In dealing with such broad considerations, we are obviously talking about the need for a major cultural change and the development of a style of living other than the one we have grown accustomed to in the United States. This kind of shift is already being initiated by several current crises regarding ecology, energy, the world food supply, and human community. But major social changes take place slowly. Meantime, as Christians, we must ponder ways in which we may introduce voluntary changes into our own lives and into our society.

Learning Again to Praise Him

I would be the last to suggest that we have an easy task here. At the root of the problem of praise is a problem of belief, and the problem of belief goes much deeper than our sensory and rational powers. Belief has to do with the depths of our being. It involves our total personalities—loving God with mind, heart, soul, and strength (Mark 12:32-33). How can we learn again to love and praise God in that way?

We can begin perhaps with an acknowledgment of our limitations and difficulties. We cannot *prove* God empirically and rationally. To many persons, of course, there is a logic of belief. The classical arguments for God's existence—the Unmoved Mover, the Uncaused Cause, the design of things, the need for an ultimate purpose, moral oughtness—still have weight. Werner von Braun, the wizard of modern space flight, said shortly before he died that he could not conceive of

the order of the universe without positing a Grand
Designer. Teilhard de Chardin, the brilliant paleonto-
logist and philosopher, spent most of his life working
on an evolutionary model which could make sense of
the empirical facts about the universe.

Many persons, however, will find themselves bewil-
dered and perplexed by contradictory evidences about
God's existence. The existence of evil, whether natural
or human, is especially puzzling. In the last analysis,
I suspect, we will come out where many of the saints
of the Bible and church history have come out—in
the recognition that we have to bow the knees of our
minds and listen to the secret and quiet murmurings
of our own and others' hearts. As Blaisé Pascal, the
brilliant seventeenth-century mathematician and philosopher, expressed it, "The heart has its reasons, of
which reason knows nothing; we feel it in many
things." [13]

This is not to say that there is no place for reason
in religion. Reason is an aspect of our being just as
feeling or will is. It is to say, rather, that in making
our covenant of faith with God, we will rely upon the
heart rather than upon the head alone. Once we have
sealed the bond, we will proceed to apply our minds
as well as our hearts to the maintenance of this covenant.

The marriage covenant offers a suitable analogy. A
boy and a girl or a man and a woman go through a
complex process of courtship. They doubtless could not
analyze all of the physical, intellectual, or emotional

factors which draw them to one another and lead finally to the effecting of a covenant. Somewhere along the way they take a "leap of faith" which will carry them over and beyond the ambivalences and the reservations they hold. The covenant itself is made, as it were, in the heart. But no marriage could long endure on the bond of emotion which seals it. It will subsist only if both partners apply themselves with heart, mind, soul, and strength to make the bond grow stronger.

The problem we are wrestling with is that the culture we live in works against this wholistic understanding of reality. It hammers, beats, and shapes until it fits us into its mold. All cultures do this, of course, and some sort of cultural induction is necessary if we want to benefit from and contribute to our culture. But sometimes a culture does its work too well. It takes us completely captive and prevents us from seeing culture's weaknesses and faults. It obscures the vision of God. This is especially true of a modern technological culture, such as ours, where psychological techniques can be applied to reshape thought and behavior. Modern advertising techniques are used, for instance, to appeal not merely to physical but to emotional and psychological drives so as to create artificial and contrived needs. Who has not been intimidated by the fact that to be "a man of distinction" one must drink a certain whiskey?

How do we break out of the mold of our culture to discover a sense of God's will? The apostle Paul prescribed a formula in Romans 12:2. "Do not be fitted into the mold of this age, but be transformed by a recycling of your understanding, so that you may have a sense of God's will, what is good and acceptable, and of ultimate significance" (author's paraphrase).

The key lies in "a recycling of understanding," which might take place in one of two ways. One way is by education. The purpose of education is to liberate our minds. The higher we ascend the educational ladder, the more we should lay hold on this freedom, for education exposes us to other cultures and ways of living and thus gives some standard for evaluating our own.

But education does not always liberate. It also hands on the traditions of our own culture. It may perpetuate stereotypes rather than free us from them. In the case of American culture, as a matter of fact, educators have charged that the approach to education is creating a "single vision," as Theodore Roszak calls it, by cultivating the powers of observation and reason to the exclusion of the powers of transcendence. The charge is certainly confirmed by figures which I cited earlier, that is, federal expenditures for higher education.

Paul had in mind another kind of recycling, *by conversion.* He knew that, in the last analysis, God would have to break through the facade of human culture and reshape the patterns of the mind and heart. He alone can purge away the sin of self-centeredness and renew within us a right spirit (Ps. 51:10, KJV).

Many, with good reason, are skeptical of "conversions" often claimed by the churches. These frequently fit cultural stereotypes and in no way produce powers of discrimination. Conceding all of their weaknesses, however, we still have to conclude that God can and does break in upon us, the Hound of Heaven baying at our heels. He does his own molding and shaping until we are yielded to his will.

But we must not overlook the difficulties our culture hurls before us even here. If God is to break in upon us, he will do so in moments of solitude, in the stillness, as we yield ourselves to him. He does not come crashing through our hearts' doors with a bulldozer. He stands there knocking gently, waiting for us to invite him in. And it is precisely here that our culture creates the most problems, for it does not encourage quiet listening or solitude. Rather, it stresses activity. It fills our ears and minds constantly with its cacophony of sounds and activities.

This means that if conversion is to take place, we will have to *want* that to happen. We will have to make time for solitude. We will have to practice listening with the ear of the heart. We will have to bow our knees to the Father and yield ourselves to him in praise and adoration.

The churches should play a major role in the recycling of understanding. In order to offset "the single vision," they will need to do a better job than they have in the past in shaping the powers of transcendence. The fact that many persons have turned to Eastern religions and to quasi-religious cults for guidance in meditation is a stark testimony of the churches' failings. Too often, in both education and worship, Christian institutions have simply rubber-stamped their culture.

I see two ways in which the churches may assist in the recovery of the powers of transcendence. One is *through church-related educational institutions,* especially colleges. There has never been a time when such institutions were more desperately needed to restore balance in education. The purpose of institutions of higher education is directly cultural—to prepare shapers of tomorrow's culture. In the case of Christian institutions, this purpose should be defined in terms of a wholistic view of society, wherein we pursue not merely "knowledge for use" but the abundant life.

The other way in which the churches may assist in the recovery of transcendence is *directly through worship*. There is no better way to teach praise than to practice it.

Sad to say, many Protestant churches suffer from serious deficiencies in the sphere of reverence, awe, and wonder before the Almighty. Participating in worship with Roman Catholics, Orthodox, and Anglicans, I have been struck by the contrast. Sometimes, in their effort to emphasize the transcendent, they may lose touch with the human. But I wonder if it is not an equally, if not more serious problem, to overemphasize the human and neglect the divine. Hymns, prayers, sermons, and all the rest all to readily reinforce the self-centered desires we cultivate every day.

A welcome corrective would be a stronger emphasis on praise or adoration. Do we have any reason for hesitation here? God created our world. He made us. He redeemed us. He has "the whole wide world in his hands."

Our task here is to model faith. Throughout religious history nothing has witnessed so powerfully for faith as persons imbued with what they believed and acting it out. Faith is an affective as well as a cognitive reality. It should influence both who we are and what we are doing. In an age concerned with truthfulness, people will be quick to spot phonies. They will also know saints when they see them. The power of divine presence in human lives is a powerful instrument for inciting people to praise God.

Notes

1. (New York and Evanston: Harper and Row, 1969).

2. *Letters and Papers from Prison,* ed. Eberhard Bethge (3d ed.; London: SCM, 1967), p. 209.

3. *Why I Am Not a Christian* (New York: Simon & Shuster, 1957), p. 22.

4. See *Church Dogmatics,* trans. G. T. Thomson (Edinburgh: T. and T. Clark, 1936), I, 1:213 ff.

5. *The Gospel of Christian Atheism* (Philadelphia: Westminster Press, 1966); *Radical Theology and the Death of God* (Indianapolis: Bobbs-Merrill, 1966).

6. *The New Essence of Christianity* (New York: Association Press, 1961).

7. See Paul van Buren, *The Secular Meaning of the Gospel*

(New York: Macmillan, 1963), Gabriel Vahanian, *The Death of God* (New York: George Braziller, 1957).

8. (New York: Macmillan Co., 1963), pp. 93-97.

9. See Clark Kerr, *The Uses of the University* (New York: Harper Torchbooks, 1963), pp. 53-55.

10. *Experiences* (New York: Oxford, 1969), p. 326.

11. Bonhoeffer, p. 153.

12. (Garden City, N.Y.: Doubleday & Co., 1968).

13. *Pensées,* 224.

3
Thanksgiving

Thanklessness is one of the obvious characteristics of our society of abundance. It is evident in overconsumption and waste, insatiable desires for more and more, brutalizing of nature, and treatment of other persons as objects. It is a problem which all societies have confronted but never to the degree ours does.

Whether there is any antidote for thanklessness may be a moot point. It will not be easy certainly to overcome attitudes and habits which have become so deeply ingrained in us. But however difficult the task, if our society is to gain some semblance of health, we must undertake it.

The place to begin will be with recovery of the biblical concept of thankfulness. This does not mean gratitude only for blessings and favors received. It is, rather, an attitude of gratefulness in all circumstances based on an awareness that the heavenly Father cares for us and enters into our situation in an intimate way.

To recover thankfulness in practice will be more difficult than to recover it in theory. It will require nothing less than a resensitizing to the personal depths of the universe, developing a love for earth's blind matter and discerning its place in God's total purpose. It will require the practice of thankfulness in small ways.

Thanklessness: A Case Study

Some may query whether I have exaggerated the significance of thanklessness in our society. There are, after all, some signs of gratitude. Annually we observe Thanksgiving Day, a distinctive American observance, and we say our thank yous in daily life and worship. By comparison with persons in other societies, Americans seem rather thankful.

In reply I would point out that customs such as these may or may not reflect deep-seated attitudes. In this instance I seriously doubt whether they do. We may legitimately ask, for instance, whether Thanksgiving Day is chiefly, as originally designed, a day set aside to thank God for his deliverance of the Pilgrims or a day of feasting and self-indulgence. For most Americans, I suspect, it is the latter.

Its Symptoms

We cannot be content, however, simply to look at the external customs. There are symptoms of thanklessness far more serious than the erosion of the meaning of Thanksgiving Day. They manifest themselves in attitudes and actions which are destructive of a whole society.

One symptom is *discontentedness*. To a great extent we can blame this on the sales and consumption orientation of American society. As John Kenneth Galbraith has pointed out, our economy no longer operates on the Keynesian theory of supply and demand. Rather, giant oligopolies determine what they will produce and how much profit they want to make and proceed to generate artificial and contrived desires through advertising. The result is that we find ourselves constantly craving things we do not have and do not need and wonder why they don't satisfy us.

However generated, this insatiable thirst issues in an unwholesome discontentness. Whatever we have, it is not enough. Like spoiled children who get less than they expect at Christmastime, we grumble and complain. We make envious comparisons with what friends and neighbors have. Often discontent mounts to such a level that people are driven to unethical behavior—embezzlement, theft, or even murder—to obtain their desires.

Another symptom is *our brutalizing of nature*. Ancient societies did not have this problem; rather, they treated nature with awe and fear, seeing in it the operation of divine forces. The price of our advance in science and technology has been an objectification of nature which has led to thoughtless exploitation. We have even interpreted and applied biblical texts about human lordship as a license for exploitation.

In America there is a long history of such attitudes. The first settlers came to Jamestown chiefly in search of economic gain. Their descendants pushed westward in haste, eager to exploit the seemingly boundless reserves of land, forests, wildlife, and natural resources. They left in their wake vast wastelands, ploughing up the prairies and leaving them to erode, chopping down forests with no thought of replanting, decimating herds of animals and flocks of birds, and stripping the subsoil of its riches. None that I know, save John Woolman (1720-1772), worried about the generations which would follow them. Never have so few wasted so much in so short a time.

Accompanying this exploitation was a *savagery* aimed at the land and those who originally occupied it, the American Indians. Few were satisfied with what they possessed. By violence, if necessary, they would obtain more. The land was theirs; it owed them something.

A third symptom closely related to the second is *treatment of other persons as objects.* Behind this phenomenon lies a number of causes, but we cannot doubt its presence and impact in contemporary urban society. Persons, like things, are there to exploit. We expect them to yield to our demands.

Momentarily it is easy to forget that we may not have obtained what we have, save for an accident of personal history. Traveling around India, I have found myself thanking God again and again that my children do not have to grow up without adequate food, clothing, shelter, or education. There are 420 million people in India who earn less than a hundred dollars a year, and more than that number cannot read or write! As I write this, nevertheless, I find myself fussing about my own "poverty" which requires me to stay in India three days extra because I came on a special fare that stipulates that I stay at least twenty-one days! Only a handful of Indians in their lifetimes could make the journey I have made.

Its Causes

What lies behind such thanklessness? Is it a universal human phenomenon? Or does it have its roots sunk peculiarly in American soil?

Both are probably true. Most human beings are like nine of the ten lepers whom Jesus once healed; we have short memories of divine grace, however great (Luke 17:11-19). The greater the gift sometimes, the more we take it for granted.

Thanklessness, however, especially the kind which produces the symptoms I described earlier, is probably more characteristic of rich than of poor societies. The more we have, the more we want and expect. In our case covetousness has been institutionalized in an economic system.

The poor and deprived, to be sure, may also be thankless. Quite often, as a matter of fact, they rebuff those who try to help them or employ various means to take advantage of charities. The problem, in this case, is often the dehumanizing character of social aid. It deprives the poor of dignity, and they resent it. Thus they refuse to fake gratitude when they have none.

In the Scriptures, however, especially in Luke, it is the rich who are faulted for their thanklessness. No one has dehumanized them. Yet they take what they have for granted, like the rich fool, building bigger barns to store their riches (Luke 12:13-21).

In the final analysis the cause of thanklessness is practical atheism. If in theory we do not deny God, in practice we live as if he did not exist. We develop an amnesia about the Source and Creator of all. Both rich and poor exhibit this fault.

Thanksgiving in Biblical Perspective

Before looking at some ways in which we may recover thankfulness, we need to examine the biblical perspective more closely, for part of our difficulty lies in an inadequate grasp of the latter. In practice, the dominant reason we give thanks is because we receive blessings or favors. In America this has been the underlying rationale of Thanksgiving Day from the very beginning. The Pilgrims gave thanks that God had assisted them to get through the rugged first winter on Plymouth Plantation. A similar motive has pervaded all other acts of expressing thanks in our society. We thank waitresses and waiters by tipping for good service. We thank friends by complimenting them for jobs well done. We murmur thanks for things that please us.

The obverse side of this, however, is that we tend to complain and find fault when we do not experience pleasure or receive favors. In our affluent society, one in which poverty and distress have been exceptional, we *expect* things always to go well. We therefore become impatient and angry when they do not.

In the Scriptures, especially the Old Testament, gratitude for blessings is an element of thanksgiving. Thanks are offered for deliverance from Egypt (Ex. 15:1,2); power and riches (1 Chron. 29:13,14); wisdom and strength (Dan. 2:23); God's aid in vanquishing enemies (Ps. 9:1-4); the final establishment of God's reign (Rev. 11:17); deliverance from the body of death (Rom. 7:25; 1 Cor. 15:57); God's grace in believers (Rom. 1:8, 1 Cor. 1:4); Christ as the promised Messiah (Luke 2:38); and deliverance of ministers of the gospel (2 Cor. 1:11).

At times the expressions of thanks run at a low level, for example, in psalms of vindication. In the so-called thanksgiving psalms, however, we can see the solid foundation on which the psalmists built. In Psalm 136, for instance, all ascriptions of thanks arise out of the fact that God's "steadfast love endures forever," the response repeated antiphonally after each outburst of thanks.

O give thanks to the Lord,
>   for he is good,
>   for his steadfast love endures for ever.

O give thanks to the God of gods,
>   for his steadfast love endures for ever.

O give thanks to the Lord of lords,
    for his steadfast love endures for ever.

The psalmist recalls God's creative acts, his deliverance
of Israel from Egypt, his guidance in the wilderness,
and his assistance in the conquest of Canaan (Ps. 136:4-
22, RSV). He then concludes didactically:

It is he who remembered us in our low estate,
    for his steadfast love endures for ever;
and rescued us from our foes,
    for his steadfast love endures for ever;
he who gives food to all flesh,
    for his steadfast love endures for ever.
O give thanks to the God of heaven,
    for his steadfast love endures for ever
                              (Ps.136:23-26, RSV).

In the writings of Paul, thanksgiving is an attitude
or orientation to life which is applicable in all circumstances. In 1 Thessalonians 5:16-17 he gave its full
sweep: "Rejoice always. Pray incessantly. Give thanks
in every circumstance, for this is God's will for you in
Christ Jesus" (author's translation and italics). The emphasis here, as the words in italics indicate, falls on
rejoicing and giving thanks "in all circumstances." Paul
made the same point elsewhere. In a closely parallel
passage in Philippians, for example, he urged: "Rejoice
in the Lord always. I will repeat, Rejoice! Let your
spirit of patient endurance be known to all persons.
The Lord is near. Don't worry about anything, but

in every prayer and entreaty let your requests be made known to God with thanksgiving. And God's peace, which surpasses human comprehension, will put a cordon around your hearts and your thoughts in Christ Jesus" (Phil. 4:4-7; author's paraphrase).

For Paul, joy *(chara)* and thanksgiving *(eucharistia)* are closely intertwined, embracing as they do the same root. Both involve attitudes based on the confidence that God's love never lets us down. Notice that Paul did not say, "Rejoice and give thanks for every circumstance or for whatever happens to you." He was not a sadist or fatalist. He did not believe that God directly wills evil that greater good may come from it (as John Calvin did). No—he said, "Rejoice and give thanks in every circumstance."

It is important to note also that the Christian rejoices and gives thanks "in the Lord." In Jesus Christ, God has shown to us the limitlessness of his love. "If he did not spare his own Son, how can anything in all the world overwhelm us?" Paul asked the Romans. "What can separate us from Christ's love?" He responded to his own questions with a triumphant hymn of faith: "For I am sure that neither death, nor life, nor angels, nor principalities, nor things present, nor things to come, nor powers, nor height, nor depth, nor anything else in all creation, will be able to separate us from the love of God in Christ Jesus our Lord" (Rom. 8:38-39, RSV).

For the Christian, then, thanksgiving, like praise, is essentially a confession of faith, an acknowledgment of confidence in the loving Father who takes care of his own children. "Even if I am to be poured as a libation upon the sacrificial offering of your faith," Paul could say, "I am glad and rejoice with you all. Likewise you also should be glad and rejoice with me" (Phil. 2:17-18, RSV).

From such a perception should flow a certain orientation toward life which might undercut our thanklessness. This orientation would have several facets.

One would be *a spirit of patient endurance* (Phil. 4:5). Knowing God's paternal love undercuts anxiety and takes away our motive for murmuring and complaint. Is this not the point Jesus was making when he called attention to the sparrows, the lilies, and the hairs of our heads? From them we can learn that, in his providence, God takes care of us. He will not let us down.

A second would be *tranquility* (Phil. 4:7). Tranquility, peace, would be an antidote for the brutality toward nature and toward other persons which are endemic of our technological society. Long ago, James indicted his generation for the same fault: "You desire and do not have; so you kill. And you covet and cannot obtain; so you fight and wage war. You do not have, because you do not ask. You ask and do not receive, because you ask wrongly, to spend it on your passions" (Jas. 4:2-3, RSV). His answer—"Submit yourselves therefore to God . . . . Draw near to God and he will draw near to you" (Jas. 4:4,7-8, RSV).

A third would be *contentedness,* a quality crucial for treating the symptoms of thanklessness. Worry about food, clothing, shelter, and all the rest may arise out of actual need. Whether we can handle such concerns, however, depends on whether we discover first "the one thing needful" (Luke 10:42). Stated another way, we must "seek first God's rule and his justification of us, then all these other things will fall in place" (Matt. 6:33, author's paraphrase).

Recovering Thankfulness

We come now to the practical part of our task; that is, the recovery of thankfulness as an attitude and orientation toward life which will result in proper stewardship of things and proper relationships with other persons. This task will not be easily discharged, for it will require a radical retracking of our thought and behavior. It may be that, for most persons in America, this will not occur unless a major social revolution, such as the change from fossil fuels to other types of energy, precedes it. What I propose, therefore, will be directed to serious persons within American society who believe that human beings can assume responsibility for the way they act and do not have to be blown with every wind.

It will help, I think, to begin with *a reappraisal of the way we understand our world in its interrelationships.* Behind the brutalization of the environment in our quest to obtain more and more lies the development of a scientific method which embodies a different attitude toward nature than was previously held. The conquest of nature required that it be objectified, viewed in terms of chemical and other components rather than as complete and interlocking units. Little distinction was thus made between levels of existence; all could be dissected and examined freely to advance the cause of science and technology. In some instances this attitude has led to experiments with living human beings, as happened during the Third Reich, and some other experiments of doubtful morality.

There is an alternative way to view the world, namely in terms of processes which move toward some ultimate goal. In the scheme proposed by the brilliant Jesuit Teilhard de Chardin, the universe takes on a face and a heart. Even at the level of the inanimate, Teilhard insisted, there is consciousness. In matter this is merely a spark. But as the scale ascends to the level of plants and animals and human beings, the level of consciousness rises. Plants have sensitivities we do not find in stones. Some experiments have proven that plants given special human attention will grow faster than those receiving only physical sustenance. Animals exhibit still more evident signs of consciousness. They have a certain amount of intelligence and can learn simple things. Human beings possess not merely consciousness, Teilhard has pointed out, but self-consciousness. They know that they know.

This alternate view has not proceeded at a steady pace. Over many ages, however, it has moved forward and upward to the level we now experience. Human existence, in fact, gives a clue to the way it is heading. Humanity is the arrow pointing toward the Omega-

Point—the hyperpersonal, God. This is a much more wonderful way to see where we stand in relation to the universe than ancient peoples supposed. They saw the earth and thus themselves as the center of the universe. We see ourselves as part of a process. We are "evolution become conscious of itself," and hence we can assist in directing it toward its ultimate goal. On human shoulders rests a heavy responsibility of stewardship.

If I am not mistaken, scientific methods are already undergoing a shift which promises better stewardship on spaceship earth. Scientists, as Teilhard hoped, seem to be taking religion more seriously, or at least showing a willingness to engage in dialogue about religious implications of what they are doing. It is possible that the turmoil of recent decades may yet produce a more thankful approach to the earth and its inhabitants.

A second thing which we need to consider if we are going to recover thankfulness is *a change of our models*. In the past Americans have admired and emulated the hardy pioneers, the bold gunslingers, the tough-minded builders of business empires, and the soldiers who tamed the continent and built its economic and political system. It is quite possible that we had to have this phase of history for the United States to become what it now is. But I wonder whether the continuing reference to these models is not largely responsible for some of the symptoms of thanklessness I described earlier.

Could violence and brutality in America be con-

nected with admiration of the Wyatt Earps, Doc Holli-
days, Matt Dillons, and Billy the Kids? Could economic
plundering be a result of emulation of the Horatio Al-
gers, John D. Rockefellers, and Andrew Mellons? Could
political aggressiveness toward other nations stem from
a subconscious admiration for Sam Houston and the
Alamo gang, Teddy Roosevelt and his rough riders,
or George Patton and his six shooters? Choice of such
models may simply reflect what our present prefer-
ences are, but they may also perpetuate values by being
emphasized strongly in the education process.

What models should we substitute? In recent years
many persons in America have discovered Francis of
Assisi. It is easy to see why the gentle saint caught
on in the sixties as American youth reappraised the
values of their society from top to bottom against the
background of the war in Vietnam. Francis faced many
of the same issues they did.

Born into an affluent home in 1182, for the first
twenty tears of his life Francis did not experience any
ambivalence about wealth. He gave parties. He went
to parties. He assisted his father in his cloth business.
In 1201, however, an encounter with war changed all
this. In an engagement between Assisi and the neigh-
boring city of Perugia, Francis was captured and spent
a year in prison. A period of involuntary solitude inau-
gurated a deepening of reflection on life. When Francis
was ransomed by his father, he returned to Assisi a
different person.

Over a period of five years or so Francis struggled

to find a calling. On the negative side, this vocational search led him to reject the values and customs he had accepted uncritically up to that point. We don't know precisely in what order the incidents occurred, but Francis showed signs of a "new birth." When Assisi prepared for war against another city, Francis prepared to go. As he got in the battle line, however, he noticed a poor knight in tatters. He dismounted and gave horse, armor, and the rest of his gear to the knight and went off into the fields. Riding along a path one day, he reined his horse to one side to go around a leper. But he had hardly passed before he pulled up, dismounted, and ran back to embrace and kiss the leper. Having at last taken notice of the poverty in which masses of people lived, one day he stole some cloth from his father's shop, sold it, and took the proceeds to the local priest to give to the poor. The priest handed it back. In anger Francis hurled the money down on a window sill and stalked off. The incident precipitated a final break with his father and a renunciation of all family ties.

On the positive side, Francis desired more than anything to follow Jesus. Insofar as we can reconstruct his first rule, it contained four passages of Scripture: Jesus' injunction to the rich young ruler (Matt. 19:21); the command to deny self and take up one's cross (Mark 8:34); and two passages about rejecting family ties (Luke 14:26; Matt. 10:37). Because of later embellishments of the story, we can't tell how accurate portrayals of Francis are. In following Jesus, however, he seems to have discovered an unusual harmony with his fellow human beings and even with nature. There are romantic stories of his taming of a fierce wolf and of his preaching to the birds. Whether accurate or not, they resonate with Francis' famous *Canticle of Brother Sun,* a piece which speaks directly about the kind of thankfulness we need to recover.

Notice in this hymn that Francis was not a naturalist. He directed his praises and thanksgivings to God, Creator of sun, moon, stars, and the rest of the universe. But we do see here a personalism which might offer a corrective to the objectification of nature which results in waste, overconsumption, and reckless usage. Francis addresses the elements as "Brother Sun" and "Sister Moon."

In Francis, too, we may see some other attitudes worthy of imitation. For him, following Jesus meant serving others. He summed up his vocation under the rubric of "marrying lady poverty." He identified himself with the poor and dispossessed as *Il Poverello.* Interestingly, Francis, while rejecting his family's middle-class mores, did not reject the institutional church. Part of his service entailed restoring church buildings which had fallen into disrepair. And he applied to the powerful Pope Innocent III for papal sanction when he started a "Company of Lesser Brothers" who engaged in a ministry of social service and preaching. Unfortunately the Church bureaucracy managed to turn Francis's little band into the Franciscan Order, something quite different than he intended. Francis himself ended up as a humble lay brother in an organization he did not dream of founding.

For many Americans John Woolman may offer an even better model than Francis, particularly because he was an American "saint." Born in 1720 in West Jersey, he grew up in a devout Quaker home. Early in life he developed a keen sensitivity to all creatures, animal as well as human. A small tragedy reinforced this perception. In adolescent years he threw a rock and killed a mother robin. Here he discovered that one act of cruelty sometimes necessitates another. Realizing that the baby robins could not survive without the mother, he climbed the tree and killed them also.

When John Woolman reached manhood, he took a job as a clerk for a Quaker merchant. In this capacity one of his assignments was to write a bill of sale for a black female slave. He did so with great pangs of conscience, explaining to both owner and buyer that he was not "easy" to do so. But he vowed never again to do the same. Often when asked to write wills later, he would write all except the clause about slaves, explaining his scruples. More than once, this led to emancipation of slaves.

Woolman himself became a merchant. His business prospered. Fearful that he might become too "encumbered" with the affairs of this life, however, he deliberately chose to go out of the merchandising business and to support himself and his family by tailoring and farming.

In 1756 Woolman began his trips throughout the

American colonies to plead with Quakers to free their slaves. He used every opportunity to leave his message. As a "minister" in the Quaker society, he was expected to speak when he visited meetings. Thus he quietly laid before Quakers the burden of his heart. When he stayed in a home where people owned slaves, he would gently but firmly press money into the hand of the slave owner, directing him to give it to a trusted slave. Many persons might have offended others by doing this, but Woolman did so with such obvious kindness that he seldom caused offense. In 1763 he stopped riding horses and started walking on these journeys because slaves could not ride. He quit eating sugar, rum, and molasses because these were produced by slave labor in the West Indies. Still, tender soul that he was, he worried about this decision lest, if too many followed his example, the people of the West Indies, especially the slaves, would suffer needlessly. He began wearing unbleached muslin suits because dye for coloring men's suits was extracted from indigo, and indigo was raised by slave labor. Conscious of waste, however, he did not discard his old clothing but replaced it as it wore out.

Little by little, John Woolman perceived that slavery, war, unfair labor practices, and other social evils were the result of greed. Some persons want to enjoy a lifestyle which brings deprivation and suffering for many others. In a number of small treatises, as well as in his famous *Journal*, Woolman urged his contemporaries to follow the Golden Rule. If we would do unto others as we would have them do unto us, he argued, we would not want to live extravagantly. To love our neighbors as ourselves would make us conscious of their needs and compel us to moderate our desires.

For Woolman these were not idle thoughts or armchair musings. He lived by them. Near the end of his life he went to England. He refused to travel cabin class, even though he could have afforded it and friends offered to pay for him. He went in steerage. The reason: The cabin contained too many "superfluities," and superfluities are enjoyed at the expense of others. On shipboard he was touched by the plight of young seamen. Poorly paid, they worked in all kinds of weather, lived in cramped quarters, and suffered unbelievable inconveniences and hardships. "Why should those things happen?" Woolman asked. Because shipping magnates want to earn so much profit that they overlook the hurt they cause others. Woolman himself tried to ease the lot of those sailors with whom he traveled by hanging up wet garments and talking to them when they got homesick.

In England, where he evidently hoped to confront the slave trade at its source, Woolman detected another abuse of human and animal life which again aroused his concern. It was connected with the stagecoach business. To make time, drivers whipped horses mercilessly, running a hundred miles in twenty-four hours. Horses often went blind or dropped dead. Young postboys had to ride outside the coaches in all kinds of weather. Sometimes they froze to death. Woolman re-

fused to ride stagecoaches, send mail by them, or even
let his friends send him mail by them. He walked
throughout the country.

John Woolman died of smallpox in England in 1772.
He did not live to see the end of slavery in America.
Largely as a consequence of his efforts, however, after
1787 no American Quaker owned a slave.

What I am suggesting in presenting these alternative
models is that we *cultivate thankfulness by practicing
it.* To practice thankfulness will necessitate a sensitiz-
ing and conscientizing such as Francis and John Woolman underwent. For both, solitude and prayer played
a major part in shaping their vocations and the ways
they sought to discharge them.

Public worship can play an important part in the
recovering of thankfulness. We must be careful here,
however, to create and reinforce the biblical perspective on thanksgiving. All too often, hymns, prayers,
and sermons reinforce a one-sided emphasis on gratitude for blessings and neglect altogether the deeper
motive which compels us to give thanks "in every circumstance." As a practical matter, it would be wise
for us to use the thanksgiving psalms more both in
private prayer and in public worship. They have much
to teach us about prayer. Hymns of thanksgiving may
also help. But there will be no substitute for preparing
careful thanksgiving prayers which offer true thanks,
neither for blessings nor for adversity, but for the loving
God who takes care of his own.

4

Confession

The most seriously neglected dimension of prayer in Protestant circles today is confession. The neglect is due to a number of factors: the reservations of the Protestant Reformers about auricular confession and the medieval system of penance, the radical change in human self-understanding which accompanied and followed the Reformation, the growth of secularity, and the gradual erosion of the concept of human sinfulness which has occurred in the past century.

Although something may have been gained by these factors, the loss of a confessional element in prayer and worship has to be viewed chiefly in a negative way. To make up for this means of purging sins and cleansing the conscience, moderners have had to turn to the secular version of priests and churches, namely psychiatrists and mental health clinics. The latter have rendered an immense service, but they have not really replaced or made up for the loss of confession, as many psychiatrists now concede. Indeed, the deficiency led Karl Menninger, founder and director of the famous clinic in Topeka, Kansas, to plead for recovery of the concept of sin and forgiveness.

This chapter will direct Menninger's plea toward a recovery of confession in prayer, particularly in public worship. In the process we will take a new look at confession in the Psalms and the New Testament and thus try to ascertain how confession may recover its rightful place in Christian worship.

Whatever Became of Confession?

Before delving into the biblical perspective on confession, we would do well to learn more precisely what has happened to it in the history of the Church to cause a Protestant aversion to it. The Reformers, of course, aimed their salvos chiefly at the system of penance which had developed during the Middle Ages. For Luther the problem was not penance per se, for which he thought there might be scriptural warrant, but the abuses which had befallen it, notably the idea of a treasury of merits and the practice of selling indulgences to obtain remission of sins. In effect, these two served chiefly to enlarge the depleted coffers of the Church and did little to effect the aims of the penitential system.

In Christianity the practice of public confession developed very early. The Epistle of James, for example, commanded public acknowledgment of sin and prayer for one another "that you may be healed" (5:16). In Christianity's infancy, such confession and absolution undoubtedly had an informal character. By the second century, however, some churches were experiencing problems with determining the authenticity of public confessions. In a time of persecution, of course, the genuineness of commitment was critical. As a consequence, public confession *(exhomologesis)* took on a more formal character. Around A.D. 200 the Carthaginian presbyter Tertullian reported that the churches in Carthage demanded a public acknowledgment of sin (of course, of a serious nature such as murder, adultery, or apostasy), wearing of sack cloth and ashes, public mourning, and prostration before the elders of the church begging for restoration. The congregation entered the process as advocates for the penitents.

To avoid embarrassment for offenders, Origen proposed private confession, which eventually supplanted the earlier practice. By about A.D. 300, after some frightful lapses in the persecution under the Emperor Decius (around A.D. 250) and again under the Emperor Diocletian (around A.D. 303-4) and as Christianity incorporated more and more persons of dubious commitment, still more stringent practices emerged. In Asia Minor there appeared a system involving grades or degrees of penance which exacted heavier or lighter penalties according to the seriousness of the offense.

A murderer, for instance, might spend up to fifty years going through the five stages of penance and be restored only at death.

This system, designed chiefly to raise the level of commitment as virtually the whole empire converted to Christianity, proved unworkable and, in practice, simply passed out of existence after the fourth century. The Latin-speaking churches, as a matter of fact, never adopted it, preferring instead a more direct system of repentance, confession, and absolution.

The West, however, did develop a system of indulgences for sin. This was connected with the Roman custom of "making satisfaction" for offenses. In the era of Charlemagne, penitential books were published with lists of "satisfactions" for various offenses. Out of this came the custom of offering money substitutes and thence the system of indulgences.

The system against which Luther protested represented an amplification of the worst features. In essence, as practiced in his day, it took away real responsibility for sins and, in the long run, promised no real remedy for sin and guilt, as Luther himself learned by personal experience. The famous preacher, Johann Tetzel, claimed that indulgences not only obtained forgiveness of present but of future sins and even applied to souls in purgatory. "As soon as the coin in the coffer rings," Luther quoted him saying, "from purgatory a soul rises up on heavenly wings."

Luther bridled at such flippant claims precisely because of the severity of his own struggles with sin and guilt. It was not sin as a particular wrong he had done; rather, it was sin as a mighty force in his life which he feared would bring condemnation. In a psycho-historical study of Luther, Erik Erikson has laid bare some of the roots of Luther's guilt in his childhood, especially the severity of his parents and their ambitions for him.[1] But whatever its source, Luther did not find relief in the juridical system of penance which the Church used in his day. Not even the rigors of a monastic career could obliterate the guilt. He found help only in the promise of Scriptures, which he studied intensely after about 1510; above all, Romans 1:17: "The just shall live by faith" (KJV). For Luther this discovery negated the whole system of penance and, more serious still, the authority of the papacy or the Church to forgive sins. The pope could do for sinners what other simple Christians could—namely, pray for them.

Within Protestant churches, as a result of Luther's experience, confession fell on hard times. The Reformers unanimously rejected the system of penance and the practice of private confession. Though Luther and Calvin left a small place for absolution in public worship, they essentially abandoned confession altogether. The Protestant emphasis on preaching virtually eliminated the priestly element of worship.

So strong was the Protestant reaction against the ecclesiastical abuses of confession that, save for Søren Kierkegaard's concern for recovery of confession, it has been only in the past few decades that Protestants have found some place again for confession within the church's ministry. They have done so out of a growing perception that Protestant ministry had a serious deficiency. Some studies had in fact shown that Roman Catholics fared much better psychologically in stressful modern settings than their Protestant counterparts because of confession. As a result, Protestant pastoral care developed to do in a slightly different way what priests had done in confessional booths.

Many Protestant Christians, however, do not utilize the skills of expert pastoral counselors or psychiatrists, save in connection with public worship or classes in pastoral education. Yet, if modern psychiatry has proven anything, it is that all persons need the opportunity for confession. There is no sense here to talk of returning to prayer booths and private auricular confession, which Roman Catholics recently abandoned. But we can recover something of the experience of the early Christians, namely, the confessional dimension of prayer both in private and in public worship.

Confession in Biblical Perspective

The two elements which stand out in key biblical passages on confession are the greater importance of authentic confession than of sinlessness (since all persons sin) and the readiness of God's forgiveness. Both points are quite clearly made in the pair of psalms traditionally ascribed to David following his adulterous liaison with Bathsheba (Pss. 51 and 32). Since they figure prominently in Jesus' teaching and ministry, we will not spend time trying to reconstruct the context or explain the content of those famous prayers of confession.

It has long been recognized that Jesus directed his ministry to the outcasts and sinners of Jewish society. In doing so, he was continuing the prophetic message of John the Baptist which called for thorough-going repentance on the part of all persons in Jewish society, including the devout and upright, in view of the near inbreak of the messianic kingdom. Baptism was to serve as a sign of God's forgiveness of sinners on the basis of such repentance.

Neither John's nor Jesus' ministry, though popular with the masses, set well with Jewish religious leaders, who prided themselves on their adherence to the revealed will of God, that is, the Torah. Jesus had to defend his mission and message, one which had good roots in parts of the Old Testament but not necessarily in all of it, against increasingly severe attacks. His chief defense weapons were parables, many of which hit home directly on this point. In a very real sense Luther's great contribution centered on his rediscovery of the centrality of this issue in Jesus' teaching, which he encapsulated in the concept of "gospel versus law."

We find more of these parables on God's mercy to repentant sinners in the Gospel according to Luke than in the other three Gospels, showing a special Lucan concern and probably the influence of the apostle Paul. The same teaching, nevertheless, appears in all of the Gospels and doubtless goes back to Jesus himself. The parables of the lost sheep (Matt. 18:10-14), the lost coin, and the prodigal son (Luke 15) pressed home the same point. God rejoices more over the repentant sinner than over those who can justify themselves.

The parable of the prodigal son, or as some have labeled it, of the loving father, forcefully depicted the father's acceptance of authentic confession, no matter what the sin. It is this change of heart which evokes compassion, and in turn, the father's compassion which evokes deeper confession. Observe the heart of the story: The distressed youth, finally recognizing the desperateness of his situation, resolved to lay aside his pride and arrogance and to return to beg forgiveness and acceptance only as a hired servant. The father, spying him coming, did not wait to hear the confession but ran and tearfully embraced and kissed the errant one. Echoing Psalm 51:4, the son only then had a chance to confess, "Father, I have sinned against heaven and before you; I am no longer worthy to be called your son" (Luke 15:18,21, RSV). Then came the hilarious celebration to show the joy over the return of the prodigal.

The same point is sharpened still more in the parable of the Pharisee and the tax collector (Luke 18:9-14). By naming a Pharisee explicitly, Jesus left no room for doubt concerning the direction of his apologia. In this way he posed the issue from the opposite side, as he had in the second half of the parable of the prodigal, namely, how assumed self-righteousness creates and obstacle for establishing a genuine relationship with God. The Pharisee mistakenly supposed that he could rest on his deeds as an assured basis of acceptance. The tax collector knew he had no ground to stand on. He had to throw himself completely upon God's mercy, as the sinner of Psalm 51 did.

These perspectives are so well confirmed in Jesus' teaching that we do not need to elaborate further here. We should note briefly, however, that they pervade most early Christian writings as well and supplied the motive for the practice of confession.

Of all other New Testament authors the apostle Paul, for obvious reasons, centered his understanding of Jesus' teaching and ministry more squarely on the idea of justification by grace through faith than any other. Prior to conversion, of course, Paul had been one of those Pharisees who bitterly opposed Jesus' teaching about God's grace for sinners. His conversion directly involved the acknowledgment of the truth of Jesus' teaching. Salvation depends not on works, he argued again and again with his one-time colleagues, but on God's gracious love extended to all who rest themselves upon his mercy, for all have sinned. None can be righteous unless God makes that so, as he has done in Jesus Christ (see especially Rom. 3:21-26).

The author of 1 John applied this point in a rather different context—against some Christian or quasi-Christian groups who supposed themselves to be sinless. No one, he insisted, not even the Christian can make such a claim. To do so is to deceive ourselves and deviate from the truth. It is also to make Jesus a liar because he taught otherwise. Here, then, is where confession assumes a peculiar importance for the Christian. "If we confess our sins, God sticks by his promise and plays fair, so that he forgives us our sins and cleanses us from every stain of unrighteousness" (1 John 1:9; author's paraphrase). Observe again how the classic psalm texts intrude, in this case Psalm 32:5.

Whether the writer of this letter had public confession in mind cannot be determined. The Epistle of James (5:16) and other early writings such as the Shepherd of Hermas, probably composed about A.D. 140, show that some churches did develop this custom early. Latent within such a practice are certain dangers discussed in the preceding section of this chapter. Above all, we will want to avoid turning confession into a juridicial system, for that would stand squarely in opposition to what confession aims to do. The purpose of this prayer is to open ourselves as we are, sinners who have done nothing and can do nothing to justify themselves, to God's love and mercy. We can do this more readily in private and public prayer than in any other way. The key, as Jesus made clear in the parable of the Pharisee and the tax collector, lies in our attitude.

These Things We Confess

I am afraid, however, that it is our attitude which poses the biggest stumbling block to the recovery of authentic confession. The fact is, the concept of sin has done a disappearing act in modern technological societies, and it has taken with it the motive for confession and repentance.

In his important book *Whatever Became of Sin?* Karl Menninger has done a case history of sin's disappearance and pointed up some of the negative consequences for our society.[2] We should probably begin earlier than Menninger has, namely with the development of modern psychiatry by Sigmund Freud, by noting the impact of modern scientific method on human self-understanding. This method posited the final means for ascertaining truth in the individual equipped with the powers of empirical observation and analytical reason. Associated with the self-confidence which the application of human sciences gave was a growing suspicion of human fallibility and sin. If we view human behavior objectively, the reasoning went, we should not make moral judgments about the rightness or wrongness of it.

This line of reasoning surfaced forcefully in the late nineteenth century in the work of Freud and his students. Freud treated human behavior which did not fit into accepted social standards in a wholly nonjudgmental fashion. What had been labeled *sin* thus became at best, unorthodox behavior and at worst, diseases of the mind. The same rationale carried over to the social and behavioral sciences. Margaret Mead, for instance, in *Coming of Age in Samoa,* sought maximum objectivity in describing the primitive culture she lived in for many years without the usual judgments by "Christian" mores.

The net result of the disappearance of sin has been mixed, according to Menninger. Although it has lifted the moral obliquities often loaded upon the mentally ill, for example, it has also weakened our ability to deal with the sense of guilt which often underlies mental illnesses. What was once labeled sin, moreover, is now labeled crime, and social punishments are visited upon offenders without an equal concern for forgiveness and reconciliation. Finally, irresponsible social behavior is shrugged off by way of collective irresponsibility. "Everybody does it. Why should I take the blame?" Thus the Holocaust and the bombing of Hiroshima and Nagasaki leave no burden of guilt since they were the society's and not the individual's decision. The Nürnberg trials convinced some, but most of the persons tried for Nazi war crimes defended themselves on the grounds that they acted under orders. So also did Lieutenant William Calley when tried for the My Lai massacre.

One of the surprising things about all of this is that, under this social steamroller, sin has also been flattened out in the churches. During the 1960s, secular theology in particular tried to discredit the traditional Christian understanding of human nature and to substitute an optimistic one. Although this kind of debate has frequently taken place in the history of Christianity, the wholly optimistic view had never gotten as much reinforcement or obtained such wholehearted endorsement in Christian circles. In a poll which I took of Presbyterian seminarians in one class, I found that not a single one believed in human sinfulness; this from heirs of John Calvin, who perhaps made too much of human fallenness!

I suspect that a great part of our problem here stems from reaction to a distorted view of sin, and recovery of the concept will necessitate getting a better grasp of the biblical view. In the latter, sin is not a matter of particular wrongs which a person does, although the plural sometimes designates these. In Paul's writings sin is essentially a power which grips human beings and prevents them from acting responsibly. Note Romans 7:19: "For I do not do the good that I want to do, but rather I do that evil which I don't want to do" (author's translation). Not all early Christian writers would give the existential nuance Paul gave it, but the prevailing biblical perspective may be summarized as follows:

God created human beings with a level of self-consciousness which would enable them to act responsibly concerning their relationship to him, to one another, and to the created order. Sin rests in a failure to accept this responsibility. The result of this failure is a state of alienation which can only be overcome by doing an about-face. Sin can only be evaluated in particular situations as the failure to act responsibly.

Judging in this light, Christians today need to rethink the way they apply the term *sin*. Irresponsible actions in an earlier day may not have the same significance today. In the frontier era, for instance, Christian churches perhaps rightly aimed their salvos at drunkenness, gambling, dueling, and various individual faults. Today, though some of these activities still remain problematic, it is doubtful whether they constitute the most serious issues for which we need to confess our sins. And unless Christians get on target here, we may speak without force.

In the last analysis, of course, it is not verbal confession which matters. What matters is whether we live and act responsibly. At the same time, however, confession in prayer and worship may play an important role in conditioning and conscientizing us for responsible action. It is a terrifying thing to fall into the hands of the living God, to experience the love which both remonstrates and forgives at the same time, and to feel ourselves swept up into his embrace where we must see the world through his eyes. Out of that kind of encounter we find ourselves saying, "We are people of unclean lips, for our eyes have seen the Lord of hosts" (Isa. 6:5, author's paraphrase). It is, after all, from the heart that we do what is right, and it is our hearts which must first undergo the Refiner's fire.

What, then, do we confess? In what ways have we acted irresponsibly? In what ways have we tried to escape responsibility by collective irresponsibility?

Each of us will have to ponder particular circumstances and responsibilities. In making confession it is important not to keep harping on our failings, not to deepen rather than lighten a burden of guilt. So you have acted irresponsibly. Admit it. Then resolve to do better next time. "Forget what is behind. Press on toward the mark of God's upward call in Christ Jesus" (Phil. 3:13-14, author's paraphrase). Could those words have meant more to anyone than the persecutor turned apostle who penned them?

At the same time there are some matters which need to enter into the confession of us all in this society of abundance. In magnitude and scope we have surpassed all generations in some types of irresponsibility. These should constantly enter our public and private confession.

Overconsumption and waste. Do we not have to ask the question enconomist Frances Moore Lappe has put to us: "Can we be the first generation of world citizens who can see that a system which turns protein into manure and generates unnecessary death both from overconsumption and underconsumption must be reconstructed?" [3] The statement cuts many ways. We who make up 6 percent of the world's population consume 30 percent or more of all energy, eat 50 percent of all food, and amass over half of the waste produced annually. Will we go on in collective irresponsibility?

Economic plundering and greed. We do not bear complete responsibility for our economic system. To explain how it came to operate the way it does would require volumes. But do we not share responsibility, as individuals and as a society, for some of its plundering effects for persons in other countries? What does it cost others that I want more and more goods and services for myself, that I demand continuous escalation of my country's gross national product? Is this not a motivating factor in the exploitation of labor in under-developed countries by multinational corporations controlled by Americans? Was John Woolman not right, after all, when he said that much economic injustice, such as slavery in his day or inadequate pay for employment in ours, comes from our greed?

In this realm I suspect that many of us find ourselves in the frame of mind Augustine was in when he could not or would not put his sex drive under control. Where he prayed, "Give me continence, O Lord, but not yet," we pray, "Deliver us from our greed and desire for luxuries which we do not need, O Lord, but not yet!" What "earthquake" will it take to liberate us?

Inequitable distribution of goods. Once again, we cannot shoulder all the blame for the poverty of masses, but can we, for that reason, shrug off responsibility altogether? Most Americans, living in a land of immense natural abundance, can scarcely grasp the poverty of some other nations. The figures stare us squarely in the face. The average per capita income in Bangladesh is about $80, that in India about $150, up from $100. Those who suffer most from such deprivation are children. In India the infant mortality rate is 122 per thousand, down from 139 per thousand in 1960. As a result of malnutrition, children are overly susceptible to diseases, often lose their sight wholly or in part, suffer mental as well as physical retardation, and experience numerous other handicaps.

It is easy enough to rationalize here so as to put off our responsibility. We are all aware that India, a nation geographically about a third the size of the United States, is vastly overpopulated with 630 million inhabitants. If the Indians were to reduce their population, we can say, they would have no problem. To some extent that is true, and the people of India are working on that problem where they are part of the problem. Does that excuse you and me from working at a solution to this problem where we can contribute to a solution, that is, in cutting down our accumulation of wealth and sharing with underdeveloped nations? Can we turn our heads away when we see the heavenly Father bending over the heads of each of his children as they die of malnutrition, cold, disease, and other things? Or will we hear Christ repeat those accusing words, "I was hungry and you gave me nothing to eat; I was thirsty and you gave me nothing to drink; I was a stranger and you did not take me into your house; I was naked and you did not provide clothes for me; I was sick and imprisoned, and you did not visit me" (Matt. 25:42-43, author's paraphrase). I shudder to think so.

Egocentric, convenience-centered life-styles. Technology has brought many marvelous benefits to humanity. At the same time it has encouraged our natural egocentric tendencies and drives. The payoff has been increasing self-centeredness manifested in concern for "me and mine," disregard of the needs and welfare of others, and lack of even ordinary human compassion. The injured traveler from Jericho in Jesus' parable had only three who passed by on the other side; how many of us would pass him by in our day?

Once more, we can take a burden off of our minds by invoking contemporary conditions and customs. "It is inconvenient and sometimes dangerous to become involved. Those we help are not always grateful. Others will help. We pay taxes to secure the services others need. Someone else will do it if we don't." When all excuses have been put forth, however, they sound inadequate, and we feel empty for having tried to offer them. From somewhere comes a Samaritan to accuse us of dereliction.

Abuse of nature. Our age is guilty of wanton burning of forests, gouging out of hills to mine coal or minerals, and reckless killing of animals. It will be easy to excuse ourselves of culpability by blaming technology. We must recognize, however, that technology does what we ask it to do; it does not compel us to use it for abuse of nature or the environment.

Before concluding this chapter, I want to underscore again that we will need to remain vigilant against the temptation to escape responsibility by way of collective irresponsibility. You may think I have hammered at this to the point of boredom. Within our social context, however, it is absolutely critical that we know about and avoid this deceptive route. "If everybody's doing it," we may reason, "then nobody's guilty." That is precisely the rationale which lets many persons continue down the path of social, economic, and political irresponsibility today.

When you find yourself tempted to take this path, remember that you will not answer to or for the nebulous "everybody" but to one and for one. In confession, as Søren Kierkegaard instructs us in *Purity of Heart,* we should envision ourselves as solitary individuals standing on a stage with only one—God—as our audience. He will not be listening to hear whether "so and so" did what we are doing. He will ask only, Did you will *one* thing, the good, what I will? What would be your reply?

Notes

1. *Young Man Luther* (New York: W. W. Norton, 1958).

2. Karl Menninger, *Whatever Became of Sin?* (New York: Hawthorn Books, Inc., 1973).

3. "Wasting and Wanting," *The Courier-Journal and Times,* Oct. 20, 1974, E/3.

5
Intercession
and
Petition

Intercession and petition will be considered together in this chapter since they are slight variations of the same form and thus pose the same questions about prayer. Intercession is actually a special kind of petition, a petition offered on behalf of another person or other persons and events.

Consideration of these forms brings us to the crux of our reaffirmation of prayer in the modern day, for no traditional aspect of prayer has been and is subjected to more serious skepticism than intercession or petition. To be sure, few persons dispute that prayers of intercession or petition may influence the person who prays; they can find empirical evidence to confirm that fact. What they dispute is whether prayer does anything beyond the person who prays, let us say, to effect healing or to affect the outcome of one's personal history or the events of world history.

Such skepticism, as Morton T. Kelsey has shown in *Healing and Christianity,* is a relatively recent phenomenon, a product of a mechanistic view of the universe.[1] Such a view made its appearance in the Enlightenment of the seventeenth century, but it did not come of age until the nineteenth. Today it hangs on in theological circles despite the fact that most scientists have abandoned the model in favor of a more organic one. The new model leaves at least some room for prayer's effects. Science, especially since Einstein framed his theory of relativity, no longer operates on the assumption that the universe functions in a wholly predictable fashion.

Intercession and Petition in Biblical Perspective

There is no question that biblical writers believed that intercessory prayers influenced what God did. We must recognize, of course, that all of them conceived the effects of intercession in terms of their understanding of the universe. Typically they thought of a flat earth supported by pillars immersed in the "deep." The firmament, a giant bowl turned upside down over the earth, held back the waters above the earth. The moon and stars were hung from the firmament. Each morning the sun came out of a tent in the East, crossed the sky, and receded into a tent in the West. God, conceived on analogy to human beings, directed the whole process. To cause rain, he opened the windows of heaven; to stop the rain, he closed them. He could intervene at will in the affairs of nature or history.

We must not look for complete consistency, however, for the Scriptures were composed over many centuries. Early writers would tend, therefore, to view God's response to intercession much more on analogy to human models than later writers.

When we come to the teaching of Jesus, we find him placing the accent on confidence in the paternal providence of God. He rejected piling up words in prayer "like the Gentiles" on the grounds that the heavenly Father already knows what we need before we ask (Matt. 6:7-8,32; Luke 12:30). Anxiety in prayer, as in other things, is really an evidence of faithlessness or smallness of faith. At the same time Jesus urged boldness in approaching God, knowing that, like a human father, he would not deny his children what they needed (Matt. 7:7-12; Luke 11:9-13).

Some statements of Jesus about prayer pose very difficult problems, especially when taken literally. In response to the disciples' amazement at the withering of the fig tree, he said, "Have faith in God. Truly, I say to you, whoever says to this mountain, 'Be taken up and cast into the sea,' and does not doubt in his heart, but believes that what he says will come to pass, it will be done for him. Therefore I tell you, whatever you ask in prayer, believe that you receive it, and you will" (Mark 11:22-23, RSV). In Matthew, Jesus made essentially the same response to the disciples' puzzlement that he had healed an epileptic child when they could not. The reason for their impotence was their "little faith." "For truly, I say to you, if you have faith as a grain of mustard seed, you will say to this mountain, 'Move hence to yonder place,' and it will move; and nothing will be impossible to you" (Matt. 17:20-21, RSV; see Luke 17:6; 1 Cor. 13:2).

Faith healers regularly invoke these passages in promoting their healing efforts. On the one side, Jesus' words provide a convenient explanation if someone is not healed, namely, lack of faith (usually of the patient and not of the healer). On the other side, they offer an incentive for trying even when some cases seem beyond help. I read of one faith healer, for example, who claimed to obtain sight for a child born without eye sockets!

I am not sure anyone will ever find the true key to these statements. They are obviously hyperbolic. The main point, however, coincides with Jesus' teaching elsewhere: Above all else, we must trust God. Is that not what a grain of mustard seed (just as the birds, lilies, or hairs of our head) teaches us? It betrays no anxiety. It lets God do with it as he wills. Certainly it is unlikely in the extreme that Jesus believed we could manipulate God anyway we wanted to if we had enough faith. The fact is, if we had enough faith, we wouldn't pester God with impossible demands; we would know he cared enough to do what, as a loving Father, he saw we needed (Matt. 7:7-11).

The apostle Paul discovered that God doesn't always answer prayers the way we want him to, no matter how much faith and determination we may have. We don't know what Paul's "thorn in the flesh" was. In the Corinthian letters there are evidences of some kind of eye trouble (see also Acts 9:18) which disfigured his face and made him unsightly and also of epilepsy. Whatever it was, it distressed him immensely: "I exhorted the Lord three times about this," he said, "that he take it away from me" (2 Cor. 12:8; author's translation). "Three times" would mean in Hebrew idiom that Paul did everything he could; he pulled out all the stops.

But he did not get the answer he wanted, physical healing. Instead, he heard the answer to "unanswered" prayers, "My grace is sufficient for you, for my power is perfected in weakness" (2 Cor. 12:9, author's paraphrase). That, of course, is never the answer we want. We want to be self-sufficient, without dependency. But when we come up against those situations with which we cannot cope on our own, these are the only words which will suffice. In the "depths" of life we will hear them.

So John Bunyan discovered. Growing up in Puritan England in the seventeenth century, Bunyan (1628-1688) developed a hypersensitive religious conscience. He became almost a manic depressive trying to discover, as all Puritans had to, whether he was among the "elect." His moods went up and down like a thermometer. One time he would hear a reassuring text of Scriptures; another time he would hear an accusing one. He feared he had committed the unpardonable sin, that he had sold his Christian birthright, that he had denied Christ. Then one day, worshiping with the little Baptist congregation at Bedford, these words came into his mind three times. Later he described their impact: "Oh! methought that every word was a mighty word unto me; as *my*, and *grace*, and *sufficient*, and *for thee;* they were then, and sometimes are still, far bigger than others be." [2] He reflected the experience in the title of his autobiography, *Grace Abounding to the Chief of Sinners*.

Many, of course, will not understand the rationale Paul gave for this: "For my power is made perfect in weakness" (2 Cor. 12:9, RSV). Our logic runs: The weak are weak; the strong are strong. Here Paul defied our logic by saying, "In weakness there is strength." He had in mind the message of the cross. He knew that there is a power which we can tap into if we will, the power which raised Christ from the dead. But we only learn what that power can do in the "depths," when we have exhausted our own resources. For those who learn this there is no contradiction in saying, "When I am weak, then I am strong" (2 Cor. 12:10, RSV).

The fact that Paul was not healed, of course, raises an intriguing question: Why not? If God sometimes brings physical or other aid, why not this time? We cannot answer that question fully; Paul certainly didn't try to. We should notice, however, that Paul did not blame God for his affliction. Rather, it was "Satan's messenger." All too often people will resort to a glib fatalism when tragedy strikes. "It must have been

God's will." I heard someone make that very comment when two 747s collided on the Canary Islands, taking over 550 lives. Paul would not accept this view of evil. He knew evil is something of a mystery. In the natural order, floods and earthquakes would be consequences of the unfinished nature of the universe. In the human order evil would be due to the freedom God has granted. God allows evil; he does not cause it. Various factors may affect the way we behave, but we cannot blame our misbehavior directly on God. We can choose good or evil.

Why, then, did God not take away Paul's "thorn in the flesh?" Could it be because he couldn't without violating the principle of freedom he has established? To allow us to have this freedom, God had to limit himself. This does not mean that he will not eventually triumph; that he will is the promise of the Scriptures. But he has chosen to do so by the gentle persuasion of love rather than by violence. Consequently, he allows himself to be edged out on a cross, sharing in the suffering brought by evil. And to those who enter into suffering with him he shares his power of resurrection. As the apostle would put it, "In weakness we find God's power" (2 Cor. 12:10). Nothing really matters, then, except "to know him, and the power of his resurrection, and to share in his sufferings, conforming ourselves to his death," that perchance we may "attain to the resurrection which is from the dead" (Phil. 3:10 f., author's translation).

So we must not put God on the spot by expecting

him to grant every whim as a sign of faith. That kind of testing is really a confession of unfaith. So John Bunyan decided when he started to see whether he had real faith by praying for God to dry up some mud puddles.[3]

Still to be considered, however, are clear asseverations in Scriptures that prayer is effective beyond the person praying. Indeed, we seldom find any interest in the impact of prayer on the latter. Quite to the contrary, it is assumed implicitly or explicitly that God hears and responds to the pleas of his children.

The most explicit assertion of this is found in James 5:13-18, where James developed an argument on the power of prayer. The passage deserves quotation and exposition.

> Is any one among you suffering? Let him pray. Is any cheerful? Let him sing praise. Is any among you sick? Let him call for the elders of the church, and let them pray over him, anointing him with oil in the name of the Lord; and the prayer of faith will save the sick man, and the Lord will raise him up; and if he has committed sins, he will be forgiven. Therefore confess your sins to one another, and pray for one another, that you may be healed. The prayer of a righteous man has great power in its effects. Elijah was a man of like nature with ourselves and he prayed fervently that it might not rain, and for three years and six months it did not rain on the earth. Then he prayed again and the heaven gave rain, and the earth brought forth its fruit (RSV).

In this statement James was obviously trying to make the strongest possible case for prayer, evidently against some who doubted its efficacy. Note that James didn't even bother to distinguish prayer and God's action; the two would coincide completely. The statement that the "prayer of faith" will heal is parallel to the statement that "the Lord will raise him up" from his sick bed. How could this be so? Surely because for James "the prayer of faith" or authentic prayer would coincide with God's will. In his or her heart of hearts, the true believer would not ask something that stood in conflict with God's will.

The same applies, James went on to say, to forgiveness of sins and healing. Not just any prayer thrown up in desperation will be effective, but "the prayer of a righteous person" (5:16). Elijah is an example par excellence of a "righteous person," that is, one who truly knew God and sought his will. The word *righteous* may mislead us a little. A close examination of 1 Kings 17 and 18, which supplies the background for this illustration, will show that what characterized Elijah was his *intimacy with God.* God commanded the ravens to feed him (17:4). He directed him step by step in a desperate situation during the drought. He listened to his pleas to heal the child of the Sidonian widow (17:22). When shown her son restored to life, the widow revealed the main point: "Now I know that you are a man of God, and that the word of the Lord in your mouth is truth" (17:24, RSV). Thus the Lord "heard" his "servant" in the duel with the priests of Baal (18:37-39) and also in the withholding or sending of rain (Jas. 5:17-18). Elijah knew God's will and shared his secrets.

Many modern readers, of course, will be left with

serious questions about the original stories, but James obviously wanted to place his accent over the word *righteous*. His view of prayer helps us to understand Matthew's explanation of the disciples' failure to heal the epileptic. Unlike Elijah, they lacked intimacy with God by which they could have seen into the situation deeply enough to have perceived God's will.

Matthew consistently connected the effectiveness of intercession and petition with authentic faith. Faith "saved" the centurion's son (Matt. 8:13), the woman with a hemorrhage who touched his garment (Matt. 9:22), and the Canaanite woman's daughter (Matt. 15:28). Conversely, Jesus did not perform many miracles in his hometown "on account of their unbelief" (Matt. 13:58). Even Jesus could not control the situation in which he performed his Father's work. There are limits set by the freedom God has granted his own.

Intercession and Petition in Modern Perspective

It is quite clear, then, that the earliest Christians believed in the effectiveness of intercession and petition, not perhaps in the way this has been construed by some modern faith healers but in a very real sense. They clearly recognized the limits of prayer, even in the case of Jesus himself, set by the freedom God has ordained for his creation. This freedom is operative even in belief. Because God does not walk roughshod over our wills, he cannot always effect his own actual will. He depends on our voluntary cooperation.

What can we say about the effectiveness of intercession and petition today? Does the radical shift in our modern world view and self-understanding even allow us to contemplate an impact of prayer beyond the person who prays? Or must we surrender entirely such a claim along with the ancient world view and thus give up on prayer except for utilitarian purposes?

A Negative Judgment

There are those who would opt for an essentially negative answer to these queries. Rudolph Bultmann concluded that miracles, and thus the possibility of influencing the order of things through prayer, belonged to the ancient world view which is no longer tenable for us. Since to the first Christian miracles involved an intervention of God from "up there" to "down here," we have no way to bring them over into our present world picture. The purpose of miracle stories in the New Testament was essentially to evoke faith. Moderners, however, do not and cannot believe in them. Rather, they perceive a universe operating in an orderly fashion that allows no room for the extraordinary intervention of divine beings. Prayer is to them meaningful, therefore, only as it applies to them personally.

In the 1960s the so-called radical or secular theologians adopted a similar line. Whatever may be the actual shape of things, the more radical ones insisted, prayer means little to modern human beings. What matters is action. What people once sought to effect through prayer, we now must do through our activities.

Human beings have at last "come of age." This means that, whereas our ancestors sought to solve their problems by invoking God or divine beings, we are grown up enough to solve our problems without such help. Thus, for instance, where they prayed for relief from a headache, we take an aspirin tablet. Where they prayed for rain, we seed the clouds. Where they prayed for healing, we consult medical doctors. Where they cried out in a moment of terror, we control our fears. According to Allan R. Brockway, "the secular saint" finds prayer and worship problematic. These are only vestiges of an adolescent humanity. If they have a place in a "steady state universe" such as ours, it is quite different from the one our forebears used to occupy. We can be "gods" to ourselves or at least supermen.[4]

Intercession and Petition Reassessed

To accept either of the preceding views of the effects of prayer would involve writing off many centuries of religious experience on the basis of the fact that the reports were connected with a world view we no longer hold. The points at which we have to question such a decision are two: (1) Were the experiences recorded tied so closely to the world view that we cannot trust them at all, or do they have an empirical base in experience which change of the world view does not cancel? (2) Can we find no way to make sense of such experiences and no analogies to them in our modern world view based on empirical sciences?

I would answer the first question emphatically in

the negative. It is true that stories about prayer and healing manifest a certain stereotyped character and that early Christian preachers used them to evoke belief. It is also true that such stories have parallels in other ancient literature. For example, in *The Life of Apollonius of Tyana,* a first century Greek miracle worker, or in rabbinic writings. Some, especially of the second century, are of doubtful veracity. None of these facts, however, rule out the possibility that real events were empirically witnessed and recorded. Regarding the charge of *stereotyping,* one has to ask how many ways we can report an event. Regarding *usage to evoke belief,* one has to ask if that would necessarily cause distorting. Regarding *parallels in other literature,* one has to ask whether this does not confirm rather than deny the substantive nature of the reports. Regarding the doubtful *character of some* (the story of Jesus turning clay birds into live ones as in the *Protoevangelium of James*), one has to ask if the embellished stories do not reassure us about the simple and unembellished ones.

There is need here to clarify what constitutes a *miracle* in the biblical writings. A miracle is not something contrary to nature. Healing, for example, involves a restoration of a natural function, not an extraordinary event. The miracle lies in the fact that what occurs becomes an event in which God discloses himself in his gracious activity to the eyes of a believer. A nonbeliever may witness the same external phenomena and see no miracle, and, contrary to the suppositions of apologists such as Blaisé Pascal, miracles were not intended to convince unbelievers. Rather, they were windows opened to the inner side of our existence where God, as it were, reveals his providential guidance.

This brings us to the second question, that is, whether our own experience may supply analogies and thus allow us to make sense of intercession and petition after all. If our pre-logical suppositions leave no room for a personalistic understanding of the universe, we will rule out at once the possiblity of God's involvement in directing the universe and disclosures of that involvement. That is what Deism did. The universe is a clock. God made it, wound it up, and flung it out into space. He no longer intrudes into its operation. Prayer would be useless, except for its influence on the one praying. Neither Bultmann, with his demythologizing and remythologizing, nor the secular theologians, with their "steady-state universe," got far from this mechanistic picture. This is seen precisely in their unwillingness to allow room for the effect of prayer.

As I indicated in an earlier chapter, we have begun to witness the breaking up of the old scientific picture and the fashioning of a new one. The new one, constructed along evolutionary lines, thinks of the operation of the universe in terms of a complex process of development forwards and upwards toward Point Omega. We cannot suppose, Teilhard de Chardin has pointed out, that this progress occurred because of a push from below, from the level of matter. We can only explain it by supposing a pull from the Omega Point. Stated in theological language, we have to suppose that God, Divine Love Itself, propels it forward. He does not do this, as study of evolution itself indicates, in mechanical fashion. The process moves forwards and backwards, but the pull of Love eventually overcomes the forces of dissolution which pull against it.

In the operation of this process we have to posit various levels of freedom according to ascending levels of consciousness. At the inanimate level we may speak of contingency. There Love operates in a more deterministic fashion, which we may observe and categorize by the concept of "natural law." At the animate level we may begin to speak of freedom. There Love guides in a less coercive way. At the level of mind, the human level, we have to speak of both freedom and responsibility. There Love does not coerce; it woos and coaxes and encourages, like a father or mother directing their children. It pays the price of granting such freedom, namely, disobedient, errant, and irresponsible behavior. Love also suffers.

In this model we may envision a role of intercession and petition. We cannot think of a determinative role such as some faith healers claim, in which it would appear that God had nothing better to do than to sit around and wait for us to make requests. No, even God operates within the limitations he has established in order to share his freedom with us. He does not play roulette with his creation.

The role of petition or intercession is much more modest that this. I do not mean by petition and intercession simply a profusion of words or thoughts about someone or something. I am thinking instead of an outpouring of love energies on behalf of others, something of which we as persons are quite capable. Could it be that God allows these energies to supplement his own, those which are directing the universe toward its ultimate goal? Could it be that these outpourings may, on some occasions, add a little something extra to God's own efforts to effect a healing or a conversion or to do something else?

Although there is no way to establish empirically, by scientific experiment, what happens to these love energies or what they do, there are some empirical evidences which may help to establish the model we are talking about. One is the experiments which demonstrate consciousness in plants, alluded to in an earlier chapter. If love affects plant growth, may it not also influence what happens at higher levels of consciousness, especially that of human beings? A human being deprived of love will wither and fade; one showered with love will blossom and gleam. Another is the growing evidence of the fact that healing involves not just the physical body but the social environment, mental and emotional state, and even intangible spiritual factors.

According to a filmed report which I have seen on

this topic, medical doctors theorize that faith enters into healing in extensive ways since about 60 percent of all illnesses are psychosomatic. High intensity electronic photographs of a respected "healers" hands during the healing process and at other times revealed two different colors of light perhaps indicative of energy changes. It was speculated that this kind of healing may work on the same principle as acupuncture.

The theory behind acupuncture is that certain *energies* flow through the body and maintain its health. If the channels become clogged up, the body suffers illness. Needles are inserted so as to open up the channels and restore their proper functioning. Along similar lines, the energies which flow from a healer's fingers may unclog the channels and bring healing. Interestingly, many medical doctors have less difficulty accepting evidences for healing of the whole person than do many theologians.

This model helps to explain why we cannot expect our intercessions and petitions always to bring the results we have in mind. Our outpouring of love energies is only one factor the heavenly Father has to take into account. We cannot know the myriad other factors in the complex process through which he effects his will. As Paul repeatedly reminded his contemporaries, God is doing everything he can, and one day love will be completely victorious over evil. God will be "all in all" (1 Cor. 15:28). Meantime, the whole creation suffers birthpangs as it awaits redemption (Rom. 8:22).

When You Pray

The view of prayer which I have proposed frequently evokes the question: Should I pray, then, for healing for someone who has a terminal illness? My answer is: Yes, indeed. You can't help it. If you love the person for whom you pray, from your heart of hearts you will pour out all the love energies you can muster on behalf of healing. Whatever *words* you utter, this will always be your real prayer, although at times you may pray also that prolonged suffering may end.

Will such a prayer not conflict with God's will? Not at all. At least not his ultimate will. His ultimate will is health and wholeness. Sickness, suffering, and death stand against that will, and one day he will conquer even that last enemy, death, as he has signified already in raising Christ from the dead (1 Cor. 15:54-55).

The test of our faith will come, however, in whether we can pray even these prayers open-endedly, namely, without insisting on an outcome we have hoped for. The prayer of a Christian "in Jesus' name" always embraces at the same time the desire that God's will be done on earth as in heaven (Matt. 6:10). A certain humility has to pervade our petitions, a recognition that we mortals cannot know the limitations within which God works. The measure of our faith is the extent to which we can entrust ourselves and those for whom we make intercessions and petitions into the Father's hands. We, to be sure, do not have to qualify our prayers with the phrase "according to thy will" or "if it be thy will." That too must go deeper than words; it should accompany our "soul's sincere desire."

To pray with this kind of trust in God requires a level of maturity and perception which most of us do not possess. Certainly we do not come by it naturally. The apostle Paul recognized our problem here. We do not know how to "pray as we ought," he observed (Rom. 8:26). We are too bound by self-centered perceptions to perceive God's situation.

The answer, as Paul perceived, lies in the Spirit's aid in our impotence: "The Spirit himself intercedes for us with sighs too deep for words. And he who searches the hearts of men knows what is the mind of the Spirit, because the Spirit intercedes for the saints according to the will of God" (Rom. 8:26-27, RSV). Observe the last phrase, "according to the will of God." However poorly we may pray, the Spirit synchronizes our deepest concerns with God's will.

At the same time, however, we must assume that growth takes place, also through the Spirit's help. As we "grow in grace and in the knowledge of our Lord and Saviour Jesus Christ" (2 Pet. 3:18, KJV), we should pray more as we ought. Stated another way, as we grow in love, "with knowledge and all discernment," we should gain a sense of things that truly matter (Phil. 1:9-10). We obtain "a sense of God's will, what is good, acceptable to him, and of ultimate significance" (Rom. 12:2, author's paraphrase). Most of us can probably imagine ourselves sliding across a scale from purely self-centered prayers to purely selfless ones.

On one end would be the query James and John put to Jesus when the Samaritans refused to acknowledge him, "Lord, do you want us to bid fire come down from heaven and consume them?" (Luke 9:54, RSV). Or some imprecatory psalms, calling for vengeance against enemies of Israel. "For the cursing and lies which they utter, consume them in wrath, consume them till they are no more, that men may know that God rules over Jacob to the ends of the earth" (Ps. 59:12-13, RSV).

There is a brutal honesty in such prayers which God surely respects. All too often, we throw up a smokescreen over our *real* prayers because we are ashamed of them. We utter words which have little correspondence with the prayers of our hearts.

But there is also a problem in such prayers quite beyond their vindictiveness, and that is the effort to use God as a kind of heavenly bellhop waiting on our beck and call. We have here no openness to God's will, which is doubtless why Jesus rebuked James and John (Luke 9:55). Man proposes, God disposes!

Careful listening to our intercessions and petitions will reveal the vast extent to which this kind of self-centeredness intrudes. From the American frontier comes an honest and straightforward specimen directed for relief from a drought. "Oh Lord, we need rain bad, send us rain. We don't want a rippin', rarin', tearin', rain that'll harrer up the face of Nature, but a drizzlin', drozzlin', sozzlin' rain, one that'll last all night and pretty much all day, O Lord." [5]

On the other end of the spectrum is Jesus' prayer in the garden of Gethsemane. "Abba, Father, all things are possible to thee; remove this cup from me; yet not what I will, but what thou wilt" (Mark 14:36, RSV). So also the Lord's Prayer (Matt. 6:9-13; Luke 11:2-4).

There is a candor in these prayers too. But they lack the egocentricity of the others we have cited. What characterizes them above all else is their deep, child-like expression of faith. The key to this is reflected in the way Jesus addressed God. So far as modern scholarship has been able to determine, his simple use of the Aramaic *abba* (Mark 14:36; Rom. 8:15; Gal. 4:6), which comes very close to the American word *daddy*, was unique. In the Old Testament (five times) and in Judaism, God was occasionally referred to as "our Father" or "my Father," but he was never addressed with the simple *abba* which was evidently characteristic of Jesus' prayers and subsequently of early Christian prayers. Normally he was approached as Master or Lord, as an oriental despot.

The implication in this address, on which we predicate all our petitions, is that we pray with confidence because we trust the heavenly Father. Our discovery of God as our Father through Jesus Christ gives us "boldness" to approach him (see Eph. 3:12), to enter the holy of holies, as it were (Heb. 10:19-22). It is not surprising that early Christian liturgies prefaced the Lord's Prayer with the words, "We make bold to say, 'Our Father.'"

This is quite a startling thing and it is extremely important for us to grasp if we want to learn how to pray. Jesus, of course, was not the first of his people to learn that God opens himself to us. The author of Psalm 139 knew God's inescapable nearness. "If I ascend to heaven, thou art there! If I make my bed in Sheol, thou art there!" (139:8, RSV). Sheol, was, in Hebrew thought, the place where God is *not*. But this psalmist found God even there. Nevertheless, Jesus did open a new chapter in the history of prayer when he made the *"abba"* a foundation for prayer. Until we know God as *abba*, we cannot honestly and sincerely pray, "Thy will be done." Only if we have this confidence in him, can we place ourselves at his disposal and let him do his will in and through us.

One is struck in examining the Lord's Prayer by the directness of Jesus' petitions. The entire prayer addresses God in the intimate second person singular. The petitions are made with the confident expectation that God, the heavenly Father, will fulfill them.

Give us this day our daily bread;
And forgive us our debts,
As we also have forgiven our debtors;
And lead us not into temptation,
But deliver us from evil (Matt. 6:11-13, RSV).

The prayer illustrates the very point Jesus consistently stressed—that we trust God utterly and completely, even in death. In Gethsemane Jesus himself modeled that attitude. He beckons us to do the same.

Notes

1. (New York: Harper and Row, 1973), pp. 200 ff.

2. *Grace Abounding,* 206.

3. *Grace Abounding,* 51.

4. *The Secular Saint* (Garden City, N.Y.: Doubleday & Co., 1968), pp. 156-160.

5. Ross Phares, *Bible in Pocket, Gun in Hand* (Lincoln: University of Nebraska, 1964), p. 135.

6
Surrender

Surrender—putting one's life at God's disposal—is the most truly Christian prayer. It is the prayer of Jesus in the garden of Gethsemane—"Not my will, but thine." It is the heart of the prayer Jesus taught the apostles—"Your kingdom come, your will be done, on earth as in heaven." It is the prayer of Francis of Assisi—"Not so much to be loved as to love, to be forgiven as to forgive, to be served as to serve . . . . Oh divine Master, make us instruments of Thy peace."

We cannot suppose that any of us will reach the point where we can pray such a prayer by habit. Perhaps in a moment of great sacrifice, in a personal Gethsemane, God helping, we will abandon ourselves to him. All of us would hope that that would happen. But most of us will have to grow toward a life of utter abandonment to God. Meantime, we will find our prayers striking a spectrum stretching all the way from this utterly selfless prayer to more typically selfish ones.

The fact is, we live in a culture which so magnifies self-centered drives and ambitions that we get little encouragement to surrender and self-denial. Our culture values individual achievement and self-glorification and devalues subordination of the self to a higher purpose, to a higher Reality, to God. Consequently, if we get to the point where we surrender ourselves, first we will have to be convinced of the rightness of doing so, and, having done that, to learn how to submit. Surrender will not occur naturally or easily.

The Aggressive Society

There are, to be sure, acts of selflessness in modern Western society. American society as a whole gives evidence of a certain largesse. The latter came to expression admirably in the Marshall plan following World War II, as Americans sought to rebuild war-ravaged nations and resurrect their people. It appears again and again in generous programs of foreign aid, in charities and social aid at home, and in an endless array of private and church philanthropies. If much of this largesse has a self-serving character, it is often rooted in deeper motives.

At the same time there is a disturbing amount of aggressiveness in American society which militates against the whole concept of surrender and submission to another person. Deep down, this society cherishes drive. Indeed, it has built a system around ambition, a system which feeds on itself, demanding more and higher levels of ambition.

My concern is not to give a detailed analysis or critique of this system. To understand how it pulls away from the deeply Christian idea of surrender, however, we must look at some of its workings.

I am speaking here of the operation of the American economic system. This system is predicated on the assumption that human beings will act most, if not all of the time, from egocentric and self-serving motives.

As one illustration, employers try to get maximum production from employees by appealing to their self-interest. At one time, in the early days of assembly-line production, the sole incentive was monetary. Although the chief reward motive is still financial, modern employers have learned that their employees have some other desires and needs which have to be satisfied in order to get maximum production. Employees in a Detroit motivational study ranked being "in" on things and feeling appreciated far ahead of financial or material considerations. Even these motives, however, reflect an essentially self-centered slant to which employers could appeal for obtaining their goals.

A similar assumption underlies our system of sales and consumption. It is assumed that people will consume according to self-interest. When we get hungry or thirsty, we will eat or drink. When we feel cold or warm, we will take off or put on more clothing and so on. Natural needs or desires, however, may remain relatively simple and not result in heavy consumption.

As a consequence, producers take upon themselves the burden of helping consumers discover those needs. Thus enters the element of aggressiveness in advertising and selling. Sales persons experience immense pressures to increase their sales. Managerial people constantly revamp personnel and approaches to increase the profit margin. Top-level executives rise and fall according to the effectiveness of the entire operation in achieving a higher and higher level of gross sales and greater and greater margin of profit. The system is shot through with the overarching importance of aggressiveness.

Robert J. Ringer has developed a sustained argument for aggressiveness in two best selling books entitled *Winning Through Intimidation* and *Looking Out for # 1*. In the latter he has revived the philosophy of the Enlightenment which counseled acting according to self-interest. One should allow nothing to interfere with pursuit of things which give one pleasure so long as this does not interfere forcibly with the rights of others. The main enemy of human happiness is moral reservation and altruism. We should ask only whether a certain action will bring pleasure to ourselves or whether it might stub someone else's toe. Otherwise, we should go right ahead and do what gives us pleasure.

Persons who have grown up in other cultures are often taken back by the aggressiveness of Americans. This aggressiveness is now being transferred to other people, such as the Japanese, who once were accustomed to a more passive approach to life. Conversely,

on my first lengthy stay in England, I was struck by
the fact that English clothiers did not intimidate me
into buying items I did not want and did not need.
They did not say, "Of course, every well-dressed gen-
tleman is wearing this suit." Or, "Your topcoat looks
a bit shabby, Sir. I suggest you buy this one." Or, "You
must have some new accessories to go with this new
suit." My American experience had been so different
I was not prepared for this soft sell. During my own
first venture into selling, the store manager regularly
bounded over the clothing racks from his office if I
hesitated a second too long in meeting a customer or
failed to run through a list of "specials." "You won't
get big commissions that way," he must have said a
hundred times in the two weeks this temporary employment lasted.

Aggressiveness, as a desirable trait of personality, carries over into all other aspects of American culture,
including religion. Aggressive religion, not merely in
the sense of evangelistic or missionary, but on the models of sales and consumption, is a curious phenomenon,
not without anomalies, for religions normally cultivate
the opposite of this. Religion is sold like soap, bread,
clothing, and other products. Churches, stockholders
in a corporation, hand out rewards for aggressiveness
in much the same way any other corporation does.
The measure of success in this case is not dollars and
cents on gross sales and net profits but converts made,
members added, buildings erected, and contributions
collected. As far as the principle of aggressiveness is

concerned, however, it matters little how the sales force is measured. Staff members are hired and fired according to productiveness. If they cannot meet expectations, they will be replaced with a more aggressive force.

In *The Integrity of the Church* I have called attention to the dangers posed by the pervasive influence of the business model and will not retrace the same steps. The issue here is the difficulty you and I will have with the concept of surrender or abandonment to God. Even in church life, surrender, whatever our words about it, may be seen as an unwholesome trait of personality. Aggressiveness is the winner, submissiveness the loser.

We must not overlook the possibility that our society may have discovered an important truth about human personality which an earlier Christian culture overlooked or misinterpreted. Modern psychology has shown that passiveness may hide serious personality disorders. Persons who present a docile mien may harbor deep-seated hostilities which manifest themselves in a passive kind of aggressiveness which waits to spring to action when it finds others most vulnerable. Suddenly long pent-up feelings burst like a flood over a crumbling dam. Such seems to have been the story of Lee Harvey Oswald, assassin of President John F. Kennedy. Oswald, his wife Marina disclosed, was possessed of a strong inferiority complex. He never got the kind of affirmation and recognition he sought. One day, however, the dam burst.

There is, then, a wholesome kind of self-expression which is natural to human personality. Human desires and drives to learn, to exercise power, or to achieve are not wrong in and of themselves. In the Christian view they become problematic when they are not subordinated to a higher end. Human science is problematic when it pays no attention to the persons it was created to serve. Politics is problematic when exercising power over others becomes an end in itself. Achievement is problematic when it becomes blind ambition.

In the apostle Paul's view (1 Cor. 1:26-31), the cross of Jesus Christ is a constant reminder that human science, power, and ambition must serve a higher purpose. It is a rebuke to autonomous uses of any of these. "God chose things which are foolish in the world's view in order to shame the wise. He chose things which are impotent in the world's view in order to shame the mighty. And he chose things which are ignoble and contemptible, nothings, in the world's view in order to neutralize the eminent somethings" (1 Cor. 1:27 f., author's paraphrase).

It is precisely the tendency of our present technological culture to claim scientific autonomy, which poses so serious a threat to our survival as persons. Autonomous technology threatens to enslave those it was designed to assist. It is surely ironic that the very people who designed the nuclear reactors live in terror of a political mistake or a technical accident which might trigger a nuclear holocaust, causing the deaths of thousands by slow radiation poisoning. Biologists warn that experiments with enzymes may result in the creation of new bacteria against which there would be no defense. Others fear that genetic manipulation could produce grotesque monsters. Many years ago, H. G. Wells sounded the alarm which subsequent developments have in no way helped to turn off. In *The Island of Dr. Moreau,* for instance, he illustrated the pain that reckless experiments could cause for both human beings and animals. Human sciences must never become ends in themselves. They must be subordinated to higher purposes, above all, to God's purposes for humanity.

The tendency to claim autonomy which characterizes science and technology has carried over to the social realm. During the Watergate crisis in the United States, we got a firsthand look at autonomous uses of power, power exercised as an end in itself. In *Born Again* Charles Colson, the self-confessed bad guy of the Watergate gang, has spoken of the obsession for power which he developed. By age forty-two it seemed that he had reached the pinnacle of power as an adviser to the president. He cared not at all how he had gotten there. In the 1972 election campaign he was quoted as saying, "I would have walked over the body of my own grandmother to see Richard Nixon re-elected." Power was an end in itself. But then came Watergate and a realization that autonomous uses empty power of its meaning. Colson had to be "born again" to see that power must serve a higher end.

Drive to achieve—ambition—is causing similar problems in modern society. Again it is not that ambition is wrong in and of itself; it too is a basic drive. The problem arises when achievement is measured by itself or becomes an end in itself, as it has in America. All admire or envy those who scale Mount Everest's lofty peaks, the human fly who scrambled up the face of New York's tallest skyscraper, the world's richest people, the Olympic decathlon champs, the flying ace who downed forty enemy aircraft, and Muhammad Ali, the "greatest." We engrave such images on the minds of children without teaching them to ask whether such achievements matter. Thus ambition and achievement become not the means to a higher end but ends in themselves. What should be clearly of temporary and proximate significance take on absolute significance.

Many persons in our society have sensed the problem here, often without being able to articulate what they were experiencing. During the sixties, for instance, hundreds of youth opted openly for nonachiever, hippie life-styles as a form of protest against the drivenness of their parents' life-styles. Subsequently, even adults began looking for the simple life and a return to the basics. Many are migrating from metropolises back to small towns and farms. Many are choosing early retirement or switching to jobs which demand less and offer greater satisfaction.

The Way of the Cross

Against this backdrop many persons will find it difficult to think of surrender as a desirable trait of character or dimension of prayer. In a culture where aggressiveness seems essential for survival or to get ahead, what place can there be for voluntary submission, the way of the cross?

In responding to this query, I would begin by reminding you that Jesus' contemporaries, even the twelve disciples, raised the same question. Palestine in Jesus' day was a hotbed of revolution. Most perceived the options as being two—either going along with Roman rule without demurrer (the Sadducees' view) or gathering all available forces to drive out the enemy (the Zealots' view). Some of Jesus' closest followers evidently sympathized with the Zealots, and two (Simon the Zealot and Judas Iscariot) probably belonged to that intensely nationalistic group at one time or another. A few scholars have attempted to associate even Jesus with Zealot aims, but the weight of evidence favors the view that, while Jesus sympathized deeply with the agony of his people under a foreign yoke, he envisioned an alternative to both of these options.

For Jesus, the key to human existence lies in surrender to God, putting one's self and one's affairs utterly and with complete childlike trust in his hands. Anxiety about food, clothing, or other necessities is rooted in littleness of faith. So is anxiety about national security. Over against this attitude nature offers us object lessons about trust or surrender. The birds, the lilies, and the hairs of our heads—all teach us utter abandonment (Matt. 6:28-30). They don't worry at all. They know the heavenly Father is there and will take care of them.

Jesus used a number of parables specifically to defend

or explain his position to anxious activists. In the parable of the seed growing, for instance, he focused attention on the farmer who, knowing he did not control the process, "goes to bed at night and gets up in the morning" without worry, for "the earth produces *of itself*" (Mark 4:26-29, author's italics). Likewise, in the parable of the mustard seed, he accented the same automatic or providential process by which the tiniest of seeds becomes a plant large enough for birds to dwell in its branches (Matt. 13:31-32; Mark 4:30-32; Luke 13:18-19). In these parables Jesus was not ruling out human activity which is natural and feasible. He himself engaged in an active mission. What he was countering was the ill-founded supposition that any and every human action effects goals which God intends. Before we act we need to be sure that we begin with him and his purposes, not merely with our own plans, of which he may have no need. Is this not the point of Matthew 6:33: "Seek first the kingdom (rule) of God and his righteousness, and all these other things will fall into place for you"?

Jesus' teaching about prayer, and also his own prayer in Gethsemane, turns around this axis. Those who address God as "Abba" will pray, above all, "Your kingdom come," which is the same as saying, "your will be done on earth as in heaven" (Matt. 6:10). Only then can one offer true petitions. That God's will may be done is the continuous and unceasing petition of believers, other things should fall into place after that.

You may interject an observation here about the dif-

ficulties we face vis-a-vis the will of God. First, it is
difficult to discern what his will is. Second, once we
know it, it is difficult to do it. Our present existence
creates immense complications for both.

If the impressions of the evangelists of the New Testament are correct, Jesus knew this. The temptation
stories of the Gospels reflect his agonizing search to
find God's will in the context of his tortured and turbu-
lent times. There were no easy answers, and the answer
he found was the hardest of all, for it led directly to
suffering and death. We can safely suppose that he
continued this struggle right to the cross. If ambivalence did not arise out of his own humanity, his followers helped to create it for him.

The garden of Gethsemane epitomizes the human
struggle to discern and do God's will. In citing this
prayer we often gloss over the first portion in which
Jesus fully bares his humanity. "Abba, Father, you can
do anything. Take this cup from me" (Mark 14:36, author's translation). We would feel more comfortable
if Jesus had prayed only, "Not what I will but what
you will." That would put surrender beyond our level.
But when he unveils before our eyes his agony in surrendering completely and fully, he puts this prayer
in our range too.

We would do well to recognize that we seldom discover God's will by what we might call the "vertical"
route—an immediate, intuitive apprehension. Here
and there in the history of religious experience one
might find one or two examples of that. If we knew

the fuller story behind these records, I suspect that behind even these would lie struggle and uncertainty just as we see in Jesus' experience. Prophets like Jeremiah temporized as long as possible to avoid uttering the painful words God planted in their mouths.

Most of the time God's will is made known to us by a "horizontal" route—in the context of all the ambiguities and uncertainties of our human situation. It appears to our perceptions like a TV picture, just a little out of focus or snowy. Rarely can we say, "That's exactly what God wants." In retrospect we may develop confidence that what we have done suited God's will for us. In looking ahead from our present perspective, however, we can seldom register such confidence. If we are honest with ourselves, we agonize, we groan, we debate within.

All of us are probably guilty of trying to envision God's will for our lives too grandly and too simply—like a railroad track laid out before us which, once we are tracked, we can scarcely miss. If we examine references to the will of God closely in the New Testament, we will find this model highly questionable in light of the fact that there, without exception, God's will is spelled out in small rather than large experiences. To be sure, there is one either/or: to believe in God. But beyond that God's will has to be worked out in all of the complex and changeable faces of daily life, a realm which leaves little room for absolute certainty. In such circumstances, we try, as Paul puts it in Romans 12:2, to "have a sense of what is God's will, what is good and acceptable to him, and what contributes to his ultimate purpose" (author's paraphrase).

Actually in Paul's letters the will of God has to do with character much more than with particular actions or deeds. An instructive confirmation of this is found in 1 Thessalonians 4:3-8: "For this is God's will, your sanctification." What sanctification entails is spelled out in a series of particulars describing the proper Christian attitude toward sex. Peering beneath the surface of these particulars, we can see that the apostle's concern was that women be treated not as instruments of male gratification but as persons. This point stands out especially in his insistence that each male should "know how to possess his own vessel in purity and honor, not in lust, like Gentiles who do not know God" (vv. 4-5).

Paul also related God's will to character in 1 Thessalonians 5:16-18: "Always rejoice, incessantly pray, in every circumstance give thanks, for this is God's will in Christ Jesus for you" (author's translation). The aim of God is joyfulness or thankfulness, not a particular decision or action. Such a trait is applicable in all kinds of circumstances.

In 1 Peter the will of God is related specifically to acceptance of the servant role in the same way Jesus accepted it. Suffering is seen as a natural consequence of doing good. To suffer as an evil doer, of course, is quite a different matter. For the Christian it is unthinkable. To suffer for righteousness' sake, however, is doing as Christ himself did, the righteous suffering for the unrighteous (1 Pet. 3:17 ff.). The Christian should never be surprised at "the fiery trial," (1 Pet. 4:12-19); it is a natural consequence of obedience to God.

The theme of submission is the one which runs deepest in early Christian teaching. We can see this with crystal clarity in an early Christian ethical code cited in Ephesians 6:5-9. If ever there was a context in which the call to submission was put to the test, it was with reference to slavery. The institution of slavery itself contradicted the Christian proclamation of freedom in Christ. In this instruction to slaves, then, we might have expected Paul to lighten the submission theme. But we look in vain for this. Quite the contrary, he not only commanded obedience of slaves to their masters but, as "the will of God," serving them *ek psyches,* "with the soul" and "with good intent," as though slaves served the Lord rather than human beings (vv. 6-7).

I'm not sure we, who have experienced such complete liberty all of our lives, can appreciate fully the import of such an understanding of God's will. We grumble and complain about minor irritations in our jobs while here the apostle enjoined joyous service of people in involuntary servitude as "the will of God." The contrast illustrates just how radically the aggressive attitude differs from the fundamentally Christian one which demands such complete trust in the heavenly Father and his providence that the external circumstances take on quite a different meaning. Stated another way, the externals lose much of their assumed significance when life is lived from the center rather than from the periphery.

This is not to say, of course, that we should make no effort to deal with externals. If we *can* modify them, we *should* do so if *change improves matters*. The slaves in Paul's day could do little to change their lot. Revolt would not work. We are not locked into our situations like they were. We have at least some options. All too often, however, we mistakenly assume that the problem we are dealing with lies only in the externals, whether we can change them or not. If we were to begin with the internal, with ourselves, we would discover that the external takes on a different look. If we could see then that it still needed change, we could act with wisdom and insight.

Gandhi, in developing his program of nonviolent action, frequently invoked a principle he called satyagraha. This principle comes close to Jesus' servant motif. It involves drawing evil deliberately to oneself, taking up one's cross, as it were. It involves living by dying, pouring out one's life for others, serving rather than being served. Can such a principle be an option in the aggressive society in which you and I live? Or is it gone for good?

The Recovery of Surrender

We can't give a glib answer to these questions. If we recover the prayer of surrender, we will have to fly directly in the face of the principle of aggressiveness which characterizes our society.

It may help to remember that some persons in American society have tried to operate on this model. John Woolman, whom we met in an earlier chapter, applied it in his battle against slavery and other forms of economic oppression. More recently, Martin Luther King, Jr. engineered a nonviolent protest against American oppression of blacks. Many of his contemporaries did not agree with his approach. Some whites, on the one hand, opposed all protest; some blacks, on the other hand, urged violent protest. Fortunately King could build on an attitude his people had fostered in their days of deepest oppression to inculcate nonviolent action on a wide scale. Only in India under Gandhi's leading had so many exercised such remarkable self-control in the face of taunts, curses, threats, and actual beatings. In those cases, the source of strength lay in surrender. The action emerged out of the deepest level of human commitment. If violence erupted, it came from outside.

It should be noted here that surrender is not the adoption of a passive attitude toward evil. Quite to the contrary, it involves deliberate abandonment of ourselves to God for the overcoming of evil. God, the heavenly Father, divine Love, is constantly at work to bring his kingdom to realization. As we have seen in discussing intercession, he does so allowing full room for freedom. In surrendering ourselves into his hands, we are uniting our love energies with his for the effecting of his purposes. We are praying that his kingdom may come and his will be done on earth in and through us. Whatever action we undertake, therefore, it should emerge from wills made pliant before him, waiting for his leading or "opening," as George Fox called it.

Does this way not make more sense, even in our day, than the violence and terrorism which many foster and engage in? Is it not still true that "those who live by the sword die by the sword"? (Matt. 26:52). Or is genuine human progress made by brute force?

Marxists, of course, teach that it is. They would prepare the way for a utopian, classless society by violent revolution. In an interim period they would use a dictatorship of the proletariat to assure further progress toward the goal. One day, when all have learned to behave as they should, the classless society will emerge.

The fatal flaw in all of this projection is that, thus far, Marxism has never gone beyond the first two stages—violent revolution and dictatorship. Indeed, the most severe repression is part and parcel of the second as well as the first stage. Countless thousands died in the Stalinist purges in the U.S.S.R. during the thirties. Marxists themselves are now debating seriously whether Marxism can leave room for individual liberty or whether the individual's goals must always be subordinated to the state's. Proponents of liberty have little to reassure them.

It is surprising that similar thinking has crept into the minds of some Christians in recent years. Impatient with slow progress in the achievement of social and economic justice, they have stood Jesus' teaching on its head. He did not oppose the use of force, they argue;

he espoused and used it himself, for example, in the
cleansing of the Temple (Mark 11:15-19; Matt. 21:12-
17; Luke 19:45-48; John 2:13-22). In this act Jesus became a liberator and a model for liberation of the oppressed. Observe the words from Isaiah which he cited
in his "inaugural": "The Spirit of the Lord is upon me,
because he has anointed me to preach good news to
the poor. He has sent me to proclaim release to the
captives and recovering of sight to the blind, to set
at liberty those who are oppressed, to proclaim the
acceptable year of the Lord" (Luke 4:18 f., RSV).

As sympathetic as one may be with the cry for social
justice, it is only right to note the contrast between
Jesus' way and the way of violence. First, Jesus neither
committed nor approved violence against persons. The
so-called cleansing of the Temple was a symbolic action; an acted parable as it were, quite in keeping with
his servant role. It was not an armed intervention.
When, later, an overzealous follower tried to prevent
Jesus' arrest by use of the sword, Jesus rebuked him
with the reminder that violence breeds more violence
and that the heavenly Father could deliver him if he
wanted to (Matt. 26:52-53).

In this last statement lies the clue to Jesus' *modus
operandi.* He was putting himself completely and unre-
servedly in God's hands, taking no action which *God*
was not ready to initiate. The Isaiah passage (Isa. 58:6;
61:1-2) cited as his inaugural, reflects the same perspective. Notice that the task of the "anointed of the Lord"
is to proclaim what God is doing, not to foster his own

programs. Jesus was a herald of the kingdom of God.
By word and deed he announced its inbreak. But he
did not presume that he was bringing in or establishing
the kingdom. God does that. Our task is to put ourselves
fully under his rule so that the kingdom may become
evident in our words and works.

"Wait for the Lord; be strong, and let your heart
take courage; yea, wait for the Lord!" says the psalmist
(Ps. 27:14, RSV). In the fast-paced culture in which
we live, however, our difficulty is precisely in waiting
on the Lord. Just like many of Jesus' contemporaries,
we are in a hurry to change. We do not seek first the
Wisdom which might produce genuine change for the
better or result in something of enduring significance.
We rush right on to effect our own meaningless
schemes and thus end up in still greater confusion and
despair.

Supposing that you, reader, want to choose the way
of surrender, I would share a very simple prescription
discovered by all the saints throughout the ages. Begin
where you are. Choose some simple formula of surrender and repeat it over and over. The desert fathers
formulated the simple Jesus prayer, "Lord Jesus Christ,
have mercy on me." They said it again and again until
it became automatic, literally became their heartbeat.
Scripture passages could be used: "Here am I, Lord.
Send me" (Isa. 6:8). Some hymn phrases might do also:
"Take my life. Let it be consecrated, Lord, to Thee"
or "Have thine own way, Lord. Have thine own way."
Or you can frame your own prayer: "Lord, I yield my-

self to thee. Use me as you will."

The important thing, of course, is not the words we say but the will or intention that lies behind them. At first our words may run ahead of our wills. If we keep up in our desire to surrender ourselves to God, however, eventually our wills will outstrip the words. We may have few occasions to test whether we have reached such a point, but we will know when the time comes. Meantime, we must go on pushing open the door of our hearts and inviting God to come in and take control.

If we are to find some clarity and assurance vis-a-vis God's will, it will come about through this kind of process. So many want God to draw a map or a blueprint when they themselves make no effort to figure things out. God, however, makes no such promises. He has put us on our own and enters into our struggle only to work out our own salvation to the extent to which we invite him to enter. He doesn't knock down our doors. If we do invite him in, however, as the apostle Paul said, God supplies the motive and the ability to do his will (Phil. 2:12-13).

7
A
Litany

Before closing, I want to offer one specimen of the many-faceted prayer which I have discussed. Since the chief concern of this book has been the application of these different dimensions to our present setting, I will not offer multiple specimens, such as litanies, bidding prayers, spontaneous prayers, and so on. A litany with the diverse dimensions should suffice to illustrate the point and be adapted easily to other forms.

The litany given here will be a long one not intended to be used in its entirety in any single service of worship. Some elements could be incorporated directly into many different services. But they are offered as examples of items we now need to make objects of our concern if our prayer is to have relevance to our situation. Some of these concerns may have universal relevance, but many will apply strictly to the society of abundance we experience. People in other cultures, for instance, would include other items in their confessions, intercessions, and petitions.

The examples included here will illustrate the immense range of possibilities in prayer.

PRAISE AND THANKSGIVING

To you, heavenly Father, our Creator, Provider, and Redeemer,
> We offer praise and thanksgiving.

For your love which guides our universe toward a purposeful goal,
> We offer praise and thanksgiving.

For the Spirit, through whom you are personally and immediately present with us now,
> We offer praise and thanksgiving.

For this orderly world in which we live and move and have our being,
> We offer praise and thanksgiving.

For the lilies, the birds, and the numbered hairs on our heads that remind us of your watchful providence,
> We offer praise and thanksgiving.

For the sun which gives us energy and light by day and by night,
> We offer praise and thanksgiving.

For rain and snow and elements which moisten the soil and cause our plants to grow,

We offer praise and thanksgiving.

For the soil layers which cover the earth and supply a warm bed for crops,

We offer praise and thanksgiving.

For oceans, lakes, and streams without which no life could exist on this planet,

We offer praise and thanksgiving.

For the precious air we breathe and without which we would quickly die,

We offer praise and thanksgiving.

For plants and animals and birds and fish and other living things which supply us food and clothing,

We offer praise and thanksgiving.

For our own human life in all its mystery,

We offer praise and thanksgiving.

For the assurance that our lives have meaning within your total purpose,

We offer praise and thanksgiving.

For fathers and mothers who brought us into the world and surrounded us with your love in our fragile years,

We offer praise and thanksgiving.

For communities of women and men whose collective efforts elevate the level of human life,

We offer praise and thanksgiving.

For human wisdom, which partakes of your eternal wisdom,

We offer praise and thanksgiving.

For human good will and love which extend your compassion,

We offer praise and thanksgiving.

For human activity which brings both purpose and fulfillment,

> We offer praise and thanksgiving.

For Israel, your people, and Jesus Christ, your Son, through whom we have redemption,

> We offer praise and thanksgiving.

For your church, which continues Christ's mission in and to all humanity.

> We offer praise and thanksgiving.

For the great cloud of witnesses whose lives strengthen us in faith.

> We offer praise and thanksgiving.

CONFESSION

Knowing your faithfulness to forgive us our sins if we confess them, heavenly Father,

> We ask your forgiveness.

For turning inward in self-centered concern rather than seeking your purpose for our lives,

> We ask your forgiveness.

For "passing by on the other side" of sisters and brothers as they cried out for help,

> We ask your forgiveness.

For being poor stewards of earth's precious resources,

> We ask your forgiveness.

For selfishly seeking luxurious life-styles while others of your sons and daughters lie in poverty,

> We ask your forgiveness.

For eating more than we need to live and too much
    for good health while millions die of hunger,
      We ask your forgiveness.
For consuming and wasting energy needed to serve
    all humankind and not just ourselves,
      We ask your forgiveness.
For economic plundering and exploitation which result
    from personal greed and selfishness,
      We ask your forgiveness.
For individual and collective irresponsibility toward
    nature, society, and one another,
      We ask your forgiveness.
For personal and racial prejudices which intrude into
    our dealings with sisters and brothers,
      We ask your forgiveness.
For polluting the air, water, and earth in order to ob-
    tain ease and comfort for ourselves,
      We ask your forgiveness.
For frantic, hurried schedules and crowded calendars
    which leave no room for you, our families, or others,
      We ask your forgiveness.
For treating other persons as objects to be moved about
    for our use,
      We ask your forgiveness.
For letting our hopes bring despair to others,
      We ask your forgiveness.
For shutting our eyes and ears to brothers and sisters
    because of preoccupation with ourselves,
      We ask your forgiveness.
For failing to carry our part of the social, political, and

economic load of our society,
> We ask your forgiveness.

For grumbling and complaining when we ought to be
thankful "in every circumstance,"
> We ask your forgiveness.

For lumping people together in blocs rather than seeing each one as an individual,
> We ask your forgiveness.

For holding our love back when it should flow out toward others,
> We ask your forgiveness.

For harboring grudges and being unforgiving when
we suffer hurt and injury,
> We ask your forgiveness.

For misusing and wasting the time you have given
us,
> We ask your forgiveness.

INTERCESSION AND PETITION

As we come before you, heavenly Father, we bring
others before you too;
> Help them, we pray.

Those who suffer infirmity of body and mind and walk
in the valley of the shadow of death,
> Help them, we pray.

Those who live in anxiety and dread and do not know
where hope lies,
> Help them, we pray.

Those who are caught in a web of sin from which they
cannot find release,

Help them, we pray.

Those who must earn their daily bread in jobs unworthy of human effort,

Help them, we pray.

Those whose lives lack meaning and purpose because they have not heard its promise and fulfillment,

Help them, we pray.

Those who suffer the ravages of malnutrition—blindness, deformities, tuberculosis—

Help them, we pray.

Those who are dying in wretched hovels and apartments in sickness and uncared for,

Help them, we pray.

Children and women who suffer abuse at the hands of confused and disturbed parents and husbands,

Help them, we pray.

Adolescents who are desperately struggling their way toward maturity in a perplexing age,

Help them, we pray.

Youths who seek fervently a vocational niche in a time of high unemployment,

Help them, we pray.

Parents who anxiously try to guide children through life's passages while themselves struggling through,

Help them, we pray.

The aging whose world is closing in on them as sight and hearing fail,

Help them, we pray.

The leaders of this and other nations in whose hands rest the safety and happiness of the peoples of the earth,

Help them, we pray.

The persons laboring as peacemakers in the Middle East and other strife torn parts of the world,

Help them, we pray.

Those who lead industrial and labor forces and are responsible for productivity of societies,

Help them, we pray.

Those who are responsible for social, economic, and political matters in this nation and in other nations,

Help them, we pray.

Those who minister to the physical, emotional, and spiritual needs of others,

Help them, we pray.

Those who risk their lives to ensure the safety and save the lives of others,

Help them, we pray.

Those who offer voluntary service without pay out of love for humankind,

Help them, we pray.

Those who yearn and labor for a new heaven and a new earth,

Help them, we pray.

SURRENDER

Finally, heavenly Father, we offer you ourselves to be used when you will to the end that your kingdom may come and your will be done on earth as in heaven.

Here are our hands,
  Guide them in useful labor.
Here are our eyes,
  Help them see the deep things of life.
Here are our ears,
  Let them hear more than sounds we make.
Here are our bodies,
  Consecrate them to your service.
Here are our hearts,
  Quicken them to respond to your will.
Here are our minds,
  Sharpen them to reason for you.
Here are our lives,
  Let them be a living offering.
O divine Master, may we seek
  Not so much to be served as to serve,
  To receive as to give,
  To be loved as to love.

For it is in giving that we receive, and it is in
dying that we are born to eternal life.

                                          Amen.